MY SEARCH FOR SELF:

Fulfillment Brings True Friends
of a Feather

By Rev. Patrice Joy, MA

INTRODUCTION

The experiences of my life and mystical adventures into other realms are recorded in this account. My journey from self-destructive patterns into self-love has been difficult, but a journey well worth taking. Since I am connected to communication with other dimensional realities, fitting into society has been a challenge.

In these times of planetary change, we are finding our true friends and family. This book is dedicated to those loved ones with whom I am reuniting through time. I first found a support system within and then found one in my relationships. Now I have the blessing of being one of the 'Friends of a Feather' who are called together. We are those who are on the wavelength of planetary healing. Our roles in this process are being revealed to each of us.

In this text, the ultimate source of unconditional love is referred to as the Divine. Direct messages derived from this Inner Guidance from Guardians, Animal Totems, and forms of Nature are written in italics and often capitalized. Visions in spirit journeys during meditation also reveal this higher wisdom. This comes from the highest realm of the Masters of Light and is God's greatest gift to us. This information expresses that the presence of goodness is at the core of every person. This presence of Divinity within is the primary essence of the Higher Self or True Self which embraces the partnership of masculine and feminine qualities.

As this true balance of cultural and gender equality is practiced in couples, colleagues, communities, corporations, and countries throughout the world, lasting peace can be established. The time is at hand to join the regeneration of our Earth Mother as a Holy Planet in 'One Consciousness of Unity.' We are each called to instill the enlightenment of caring kindness and compassion in our dealings. The year 2020 was a turning point in our awareness that every person is responsible for the group and must work together to build a future that benefits us all.

ACKNOWLEDGMENTS

I thank my loving husband Dan, my daughter, five sons, grandchildren, great-grandchildren, and friends who have been there as my devoted fans and supporters. Thanks for listening to my dreams and believing in me. I also want to thank all those who helped edit and publish this book.

Mentors who have had the greatest influence on my work are the following:

Rev. C.J. Wright, founder of Rainbow Spiritual Education Center in Louisville, KY

Kim Evan APRN Institute for Integrative Medicine in Louisville, KY

Karol Flowers's teaching of the sanctity of all life (www.Amoriyah.com)

Guardian Materials taught in Sarasota by E-LAi-sa of ARhAyas Productions LLC.

Patt-Lind Kyle's concepts on rewiring the brain and end-of-life philosophy.

TABLE OF CONTENTS

CHAPTER ONE

BEING ME

We are either creating a crisis or connection – chaos or communication. My life has taught me that each moment is a choice to bring support or denial to ourselves. I have made good and bad choices; some were hard. I have lived a life of advantage and one of destitution. It held patterns of abuse, rejection, judgment, loneliness, and loss. My life is also one of ecstasy, joy, success, and most of all, love. Over and over, my efforts to find acceptance and success collapsed. Both laughter and tears have filled the years, but I have no regrets because I've always followed my heart.

This adventure has been a mystical manifestation of ecstasy. My life has been lived on the edge and is truly a walk of faith. It has been the unraveling of dysfunction, disease, and distrust that brought blessings galore. I challenge you to do the same. My hope is that my story inspires you to find your strength within and build your own path of peace and joy. My destination has unfolded to create bliss as blessings continue to flow. The Divine continues to guide us all as we are 'Children of Light.'

The lessons and strength I have gained have shown that painful experiences do not have to control me. I express the vibration of a higher reality that is the result of the traumas overcome and lessons learned. Life reflects the way you look at it. Abraham Lincoln said, "Most people are about as happy as they make up their minds to be." Hugh Downs later added, "A happy person is not someone in a certain set of circumstances, but rather a person with a certain set of attitudes."

This certainly applies to my life. My life story sounds like a fantasy beyond the stretch of the imagination. I felt like I was swimming upstream with a silver spoon in my mouth. My life has been based on insecurity and fear. I am revealing things from my life in hopes your life can be based on self-love and filled with pleasures beyond compare.

My Story

I was born in New Mexico and raised in Amarillo, TX. The doctor said I nearly died at birth. My life was challenged with three other near-death experiences over the next eighty years. The name my parents gave me was Peggy Jo. I was named after my mother. Her first name was Margaret. I don't know why Peggy is a nickname for Margaret. My middle name came from the doctor who delivered me. I never met him.

My name is associated with the gemstone pearl. I was born on Tuesday, and Mother told me that Tuesday's child is known as a 'child of grace'. This relates to having balance and being in the flow. Although I am often clumsy, I came to equate the day of my birth to mean my natural state is to be blessed with grace from the Divine. I have had a charmed life with advantages galore. I have also had great emotional and physical pain. Dyslexia, perceptual difficulties, and insecurity made life challenging in school.

Dr. Joe said there were developmental indications that I was in the womb for over ten months. My long gestation period was written up in medical journals at that time. Mother never did want to let go of me. My parents tried for thirteen years to conceive a little girl. I was born late in their lives in a second marriage and had two half-brothers who were in the Navy then. My mother nearly died of thyroid complications from her pregnancy, so I had a governess until I was two years old.

Mother was an attractive woman, but her looks suffered from the goiter surgery that resulted from hypothyroidism. Her eyes became puffy, and she gained some weight. She used to tell everyone as she pointed to me, "I nearly died giving her birth. I lost my good looks, but Peggy Jo was worth it. Look at her! Isn't she beautiful?" Even though she didn't intend to cast blame, I felt guilty for being born!

Mother and Dad loved me dearly, but they had a script for my life. They felt the Southern Baptist Church, four kids, and a two-car garage was the road to happiness. I heard my mother say so many times that she stopped living her life and started living mine when I was born. I wanted my own identity. When I was thirty-three, I chose the name Patrice Joy. I wanted to be me, not Mother! Consequently, I tried to allow each of my six children to be their own person.

I saw the Angels as a child. I learned not to speak of this because my folks said people would think I was crazy. I had my own experiences regularly with those on the other side of the veil. My Guardian Angels and Spirit Beings came around my bed at night and chanted me off to sleep. The Angel's droning sounds created a calming energy around me. I went to sleep to their lilting celestial songs. Golden-white light filled my bedroom. My personal Spirit Guardians assisted me daily and became my most trusted friends. They told me everyone has these same gifts if they just accept them as real.

Mother took me to our Baptist minister, and he assured me that Angels only appeared to people back in the Bible days. This didn't sway my knowing that what I saw in the 1950s were Angels. I saw healings in the Baptist Church described as the 'laying on of hands.' I didn't question the flow of Divine through my hands, and I still don't. I just focus on a prayer, and energy begins to flow through me from the Divine. White Light Masters and my Guardian Angel guide my life. I first experienced this gift at six years old when I prayed for my aging dog. After my prayer, she was friskier and didn't run into things from poor vision.

My terrier was my best friend. She waited for me at the base of a cherry tree. I climbed regularly in our backyard. She sat beside my sandbox while I built elaborate castles. My faithful companion went into my doll house to watch me dress my baby dolls. She followed me to the neighborhood store to get wooden crates for the clubhouse I was building. I thought the neighborhood kids would come over if they had a great meeting place. I finished building it, but they never came.

We had moved to another neighborhood. Yet, I still was a strange little kid who didn't know what to say to fit in. I certainly had to stop talking about my fairy friends, angels, and spiritual beliefs. My hair color made me a target for dumb blonde jokes as I got older.

I was never bored, for I always had a vivid imagination. I still feel I saw the fairies darting around the flowers as I made flower leis for my hair at the nearby park. I stayed busy with the stories I wrote. These were to be enacted if I got friends. My favorite play was about a band of gypsies who traveled around meeting interesting people. I always cast myself as the fortune teller. On my seventh birthday, I had a costume party and dressed as a fortune teller. I did readings for all the little guests to tell their fortunes. Maybe I was a gypsy in another life.

We didn't have a television until I was ten years old. We were one of the first families on our block to get one. I enjoyed the early family shows. Mother spent a lot of time behind the TV adjusting the image while I held a mirror for her to see how to clear up the picture. It was an annoying use of my time!

My childhood was magical. I was raised as an only child since my half-brothers were so many years older. Dad and Mother had both been married before to alcoholics. Dad was given custody of his six-year-old son. Mother had a son who is the same age as Dad's son. Those thirteen years of trying to conceive might account for Mother's controlling ways while raising me.

I filled the void of siblings and neighborhood friends with playmates from other realms. I lived in the fairytale stories and of course, was always the heroine. I was Cinderella waiting for my prince. Most mundane things can be thought of as magical. It made life more fun. My summers were spent at Grandpa's chicken farm in Erick, OK. Even though there weren't neighbor kids, I had fun cutting out pictures from a Sears Roebuck catalog. I constructed scrapbooks filled with dreams of my future and started a 'hope chest' by the time I was ten years old. It had a small collection of items that I planned to have in my own home someday. Summer held memories with my cousins in McLean, TX, having great adventures outdoors.

I finally got a friend toward the end of elementary school. Her name was Jane. We played jacks, hide and seek, and kick-the-can. I loved visiting Jane's house. She had a big trunk in her attic. It was filled with ladies' dress-up clothes, long necklaces, and costume jewelry. We set up wall divisions in her attic to simulate the rooms in our imaginary home. We planned to be next-door neighbors when we were grown up and married.

I chose the name Katherine Elizabeth Harrington and twirled around in the elegant, sparkling costume jewelry and long dresses. I was a fine lady of wealth and stature. I imagine I was dancing in a ballroom with many admirers. We had fun playing ball games and kick-the-can with her neighbors. We often played Tarzan in a jungle, swinging in the trees in her backyard. I always had to be Tarzan. She said this was because her name was Jane.

We played like we went to the beauty shop and fixed each other's hair. I seemed to have a natural talent for hair styling and enjoyed it. Years later, when I was seventeen, I fixed all the girls' hair before the big dances. Mother said I was Cinderella and wouldn't have time to get ready because I was getting the other girls all prettied up.

Jane's grandmother lived with her. My grandmother lived with us since I was two, and she was fifty-five. Nannie, as I called her, didn't like sharing the limelight and kept everyone's attention centered on herself. She mainly ignored me. Nannie used sickness as a way to get the focus on herself. I don't think she was sick most of the time. She drank hot toddies with an egg, milk, and several shots of alcohol to make her feel better from morning to night.

I learned that being sick was a way to get attention and feel safe and loved. The few times Mother gave me one-on-one attention was when I was sick with chickenpox and when I had my tonsils out. When I got my appendix removed, I was the center of attention for over a week. My parents weren't demonstrative people. Dad came from a cultural era in which men didn't show affection physically. I was a dainty little girl who didn't like to rough house. As I got older, I realized I had buried anger because my family didn't cuddle and have time together too often. We didn't play games, but Mother occasionally read to me.

As the years went on, I let my emotions make me sick by getting upset and burying turmoil deep within. When I couldn't take the stress of my life as an adult, sickness was a way of coping. I wanted to be seen, but I didn't want to be seen. That doesn't make sense, does it? Trying to please my mother and grandmother set the pattern of seeking to be noticed to feel affection. As I attempted to gain approval, I received criticism instead.

The emptiness of being invisible was less painful than rejection. I strived to keep myself safe from being laughed at in embarrassing encounters. I needed encouragement, as every person does, but my attempts to be acknowledged often led to attack or ridicule. I decided that I needed to be sick, pretty, or successful to gain positive attention. Being pretty wasn't enough for me, and I don't like being sick, so I was driven to succeed.

Since my folks were perfectionists, I wasn't allowed the steps of learning through trial and error. I was afraid of messing up whatever I attempted to do. My efforts to fit in or contribute were dismissed as wrong or inept. I decided to prove my worth by being productive. Fear of failure drove me to excel in my accomplishments. Sickness can be a way to justify failure. My role models were severe taskmasters. I saw the example of my mother being a martyr and watched my grandmother take full advantage of this.

Mother confused love and pity, which gave her the need to overdo for others. I didn't want to be a martyr. Nannie was a master at playing passive-aggressive, manipulative games. Women can be subtle in game playing. Mother didn't play games, but her behavior was unpredictable from day to day. She was a very moody person. She either blew up in a nagging tantrum or went into periods of silence. I thought I was the cause of Mother's anger. If I could be perfect, I would avoid the bombs and land mines of her mood swings.

I later learned her mood swings were her attempt to get Dad to notice her so he'd do something she wanted. It didn't work, though. When Mother withdrew in anger, she wouldn't speak to Dad and me for a few days. She put my sweater on roughly and avoided contact and communication. It was important to me to avoid these silent spells of removal of affection and nurturing. I thought I was to blame. I thought I could control her erratic behavior. She just wanted more attention and time with Dad. That is why she fussed at him. Her attempts to get Dad to come home earlier never worked. Perhaps it could have had a better outcome if Mother could have talked to Dad instead of nagging him. I usually got ready for bed with Mother's vexatious voice ringing in my ears. She complained about Dad working late night after night.

There were times I could see Mother's point. I heard her say, "Jim, someone else can sweep the parking lot for the delivery trucks. You don't have to stay out this late cleaning up the soda pop plant." Remember, Dad was a perfectionist who felt no one would do as good a job as he did.

He didn't let me sweep the kitchen for the same reason. He didn't mean to make me feel incompetent when he took the broom out of my hands and finished the job for me. This didn't help my low self-esteem or my fear of being seen messing up.

Nannie belonged to a church that expressed their religious fervor loudly. Dad worked until 9:30 each evening to avoid Nannie's wailing prayers. Nannie often prayed long hours during my favorite TV shows. All our religious encounters were not negative, though. Sometimes, she played church songs on the piano while Mother and I sang. Dad missed all this bonding in the evenings. He ate supper at 10:00 p.m. each night, right after my bedtime.

My parents always wanted the best for me. Ultimately, that is what any caring parent wants for their children. Good parents want their children to be happy and to find true love. This is the priority, but it isn't always an outcome that is easily attained. Dad avoided confrontations and stayed jolly. When Mother fussed at him, he would finally say, "Now that is enough, Margaret." She would be quiet, but her nagging would echo in my head.

I learned to go into a cave I constructed in my mind to get away from Mother's annoying voice. I heard her off in the distance say, "You aren't listening to me." I was in the same room, but my consciousness wasn't there. I was in realms with my magical companions. I went into this cave in my mind to retreat when I was upset, didn't fit in, or felt lonely. I went there when my grandmother rejected me out of jealousy and played manipulative games. It was my refuge when Mother spent days without speaking to me or showing affection while she was giving Dad the silent treatment. Since I felt responsible for Mother's moods, guilt was a common companion of mine. The church reinforced this pattern of destructive behavior.

Guilt was a predominant part of my life. I felt guilty for being a female. The church we attended taught the belief that the female was the temptress. Eve was tempted by the snake in the Garden of Eden and convinced Adam to eat the forbidden fruit. The church's dogma taught that she alone was responsible for getting them kicked out of the Garden of Eden. She invoked God's wrath for their 'sin' of breaking his commandments, and they were thrown out of paradise. Our church taught the female was even cursed with monthly periods and the pain of childbirth as a result of this. Women have been blamed for provoking rape and incest because of their sensuality. I believed I must be a terrible person who deserved punishment due to my gender.

My religious training had a strong impact on the development of my personality and values. It seemed it was my duty as a good person to suffer. Self-sacrifice was encouraged. I took everything the pastor said literally. I believed the sermons taught me I was selfish or sacrilegious if I took care of my own needs. I co-dependently expected someone else would make me happy and that a man would take care of me. As I got older, I got confused and mad when others didn't take care of me. I was taught to be a martyr and to sacrifice myself like Jesus. I felt guilty for being such a sinner that he had to die for me. I felt powerless to fix all the pain he suffered for me so long ago in the Bible times. I prayed daily for the forgiveness of my unknown sins.

My family attended church on Sunday morning from 9:00 a.m. until 1:00 p.m. We also went to the Training Union Program on Sunday evening from 5:00 until 9:00 p.m. We attended every Wednesday night service and went to the tent revivals all week when they were in our town. I remember there was a tornado during one of these tent revivals. The band kept playing as the large crowd started screaming and running in all directions. The huge tent poles fell among us, and the crowd cried to God, asking why he was doing this to us. I couldn't understand this either. They were praying for mercy and got none that day.

I also couldn't understand why God took a baby or let good people suffer and be hungry. Now, I feel God isn't doing this to us. God is the force of love. When something negative happens, it can teach us lessons if we look for them. Everything that happens is intended to eventually teach the lesson of loving ourselves and others unconditionally. We create lessons by separating from the awareness of Divine Unconditional Love in our lives.

I believe remaining centered in love no matter what happens to us is a part of our spiritual growth process. Some individuals are meant to live on Earth for a short time only and then return to Spirit. I feel God doesn't abandon us or punish us. We move away from union with the Divine and create problems for ourselves. Some say we deny blessings because we are trained to feel guilty. This may be true, for I certainly was. Ultimately, life is about forgiveness and personal empowerment for everyone to be recognized as equals. This is what my Guardian Angel continues to tell me.

Mother was raised in a rigid religious environment. Women in Nannie's church were not to wear clothes that showed their arms, neck, or legs. It was thought they were trying to tempt men sexually if they did. She taught me my body was nasty and I needed to cover it up. It was against their teaching to enjoy 'sinful' physical contact with a man, even in marriage. Women were to just endure the inconvenience and pain of sex to bear children.

As I healed from my early exposure to being taught all sex is sinful, I have a different concept of what sexual relations can be. Healthy sexuality is a combination of physical passion and nurturing contact. It is the union of two people melding in 'Oneness' spiritually and physically. I now feel consummation and intercourse should be expressions of the ultimate intimacy and love between two individuals. When a couple is in a committed relationship, tender touches can be an enjoyable part of a playful expression of their love.

My grandmother's religious training regarding the lowly place of women added to my debilitating inferiority. She was born before the turn of the nineteenth century. My grandmother and great-grandmother were raised in an era of inequality. This unbalanced partnership was accepted by both women and men back then. Most women tolerated extreme oppression until the first wave of fighting for equality took place.

The cultural programming of that era also affected my sense of worth. Women were still considered the lesser sex until the suffrage and temperance movements in the late 1800s and early 1900s. A female's role in society was to serve a man's needs and to take care of his home and the children. Women were to be seen and not heard. In the 1940s, women were generally told to be quiet and were treated as inferior stay-at-home wives until the World War changed this situation. Many women are still not given equal pay for equal work. Many are passed over for jobs even when they are more qualified. It is still sometimes expected in 2023 for women to trade sex for job security and career advancement. Rape and non-censual sex is a hard case to win in court.

World War II was a turning point in women's ability to be hired for jobs outside the home. The men were drafted into battle, and their jobs needed to be filled. Women were not given educational opportunities to get into better colleges until the 1950s. In some remote areas of America, they weren't even sent to school at all. Nannie didn't feel God wanted women to assert themselves. Women should not be noticed for speaking out or being seen because of the clothes they wear.

Women did not get their voices heard publicly or professionally until after the second wave of the women's movement. This was in the 1970's when corporations were required to hire a specific number of racial minorities and women. It was an amazing experience to be part of this professional breakthrough. I made a successful career and was the first woman hired nationally in territory sales management for a national corporation.

Now, more information on my school years. Even though I had learning disabilities, I studied long hours to graduate from High School with a 96.7 grade point average. The school was hard for me. I was dyslexic before it had a name. There weren't separate classes for special needs students in the 1950s. I made up stories to tell the difference between 'b' and 'd' and gave them personalities. I also had trouble with 'm' and 'w' since I had vertical and horizontal reversals. I made straight A's, but I worked long hours to accomplish the elaborate memory pegs I set up to memorize things. I pictured pages of notes for tests to remember mathematic equations and chemistry formulas.

No matter how good I tried to be, I still messed up in school. My reversals made math especially difficult. My writing was hard to read, and my spelling was terrible. I was disciplined as a problematic child who just wouldn't listen to directions. I was very afraid of people's anger, and my mind froze when I had a harsh teacher. My English teacher used to make fun of me in front of the class. I was so embarrassed when she used me as a bad example. I was trying so hard to be good. I had tried to be noticed by Mother and Nannie as a little girl. Now I didn't want to be noticed. I mentally withdrew into my cave at school when the teasing and ridicule for my mistakes became unbearable.

I practiced writing skills at home, but I was never chosen to have my work displayed. I didn't like to be singled out anyway. One day my

English teacher screamed across the room at me, "Peggy Jo, take off those cotton-pickin bracelets." She said they were nosily banging together. I wore them on my right arm to remind me which way to turn from English to get to math class when the bell rang. I had trouble finding my classroom due to my directional difficulties and was sometimes late to class. My math teacher made me stand in the corner in a dunce hat to think about how to do things correctly. I buried the humiliation of being a spectacle in front of the whole class in tears that didn't fall.

I was often embarrassed by my Sunday school teachers, too. I'm sure I was a challenge. I asked questions they couldn't answer. I did things backward and cried quietly when admonished. I hid behind my fear of attack and ridicule. I wished I could be invisible. Yet, I wore bright colors, lots of jewelry, and either moccasins or cowboy boots. I didn't think about it at the time, but that assured, I was not going to be invisible! The cultural teaching about love and marriage complicated my life as I grew older. A woman in that era should be married, but I couldn't seem to make it work out.

In a Neuro-Linguistic Programming (NLP) session in my forties, I connected my dyslexia to the confusion of what is right and what is wrong. My authority figures had flipped-flopped. I didn't know who or what to count on. In a deep hypnotherapy regression, I related, "Things seem this way, but they are that. I feel I should go right, but it is wrong. I don't know which way to go. Up is down. This shouldn't be that."

I was perceptually disoriented and had no sense of direction regarding east and west, left and right. I invariably turned the wrong way and had to memorize markers to find my way to and from school. I had to flip-flop the direction of things in my head. As an adult, I still deal with this issue at times. I reviewed my school years with my (NLP) therapist. I didn't understand the term stress, but it was my constant companion.

I dealt with my stress by withdrawing and could spend great periods of time zoning in other realms. Life as a human being was often harsh and painful to me. I didn't feel like I belonged on this planet or knew how to fit in. I was the outsider, the one who was too different to be part of society. I held memories of being invited to the parties the popular girls had, but I wasn't one of them. I never understood how they knew what to say to one another. I was afraid they would notice how quaint I was and reject me.

I feared they would make fun of the strange things I said and wore. I still insisted on following my own dictates of style and philosophy. Until I was forty-five, I was driven to earn approval and fit the standards of success that others set. As an adult, I measured my professional success as an indication of my worth. When I wasn't being the energizer bunny, I spent my time zoning in my mental cave.

Perfection patterns were my standard. I was the one who established this measuring stick for myself, although Mother and Dad were an influence. If I made an 'A' on a school paper, Mother would say, "Well, isn't there an 'A+' grade?" In frustration, I would answer, "Yes, but I didn't get it!" Mother would ask, "Well, why did you get this red mark? I'd answer, "I missed a comma, but I still did a good job. See, it says so on the top of the paper right here!"

Both of my parents had high standards for themselves and for me. Dad was such a perfectionist, and I wanted to meet his expectations of excellence. Occasionally, there were times when it seemed I might be good enough to fit in after all. The following account was a time I felt accepted.

Queen for a Day

I used to watch the show "Queen of a Day" on TV. In my fantasy world, I was the queen each day receiving all the gifts and praise. The following story is about a turning point in my popularity. All the events are true, but the names have been changed to protect those involved.

I didn't feel accepted by the 'in-group' during my third year at elementary school in Amarillo, Texas. The clique was comprised of cute little girls from elite families. I was cute and my parents had money, yet I just didn't feel like one of the popular crowd. Although the members of the clique allowed me to sit at their table at lunch, I ended up on the far corner and was seldom included in conversations. Sometimes, they even talked about me like I wasn't there. The term bully wasn't recognized as a problem, but it was for me.

Even my English teacher didn't give me the approval she gave the other little girls. The boys seldom got their writing displayed, but all the girls did. All except me, that is! I had such messy handwriting none of my work appeared on the bulletin board. Linda and Jan made trips to the blackboard with dull predictability. My teacher told me I needed to practice writing at home nights so someone could read what I wrote.

One specific day was an exception to this stigma. Our second-grade class took a field trip to my dad's cola bottling plant. All of a sudden, I became sought after! Everyone wanted to go in my parent's car and sit by me. Jan Harrison and Linda Owens literally got into a wrestling match, which ended up on the ground beside the open car door. The winner had the privilege of being in the front seat beside me.

As we arrived at my dad's plant, huge machines were visible through the glass building front. The children stood looking with their mouths open in wide-eyed wonderment as they watched the drinks being poured into bottles and sealed with cork-filled lids. My dad began the tour in his office. He showed off an ugly elephant head paperweight I had made for him two years earlier. I explained, "I was only a child when I made this in first grade." The children nodded.

Dad had always reminded me of a janitor by the number of keys he had dangling from his belt. One of those keys was the key to the key room! When he unlocked the door and revealed a wide array of keys, even Betty Thomas was impressed. Many voices excitedly expressed, "Wow!" Dad commented that 143 keys were hanging in there. I still wonder if he knew what they all opened.

Next on our tour were floor-to-ceiling storage tanks filled with raw syrup. We introduced Mr. James, the Maintenance Engineer. I pointed out I sometimes assisted him in cleaning these tanks on the inside before they were filled. Several of the children in the group gave envious comments. As we passed the bottle inspection line, I mentioned I was occasionally allowed to help the quality control inspector look for dirty bottles. There was a murmur of approval from the small visitors.

We continued to the bottling sorting section where John McMillian worked. At the time, I thought he was the most handsome man in the world. I whispered to a little red-haired girl named Mary, "I'm in love with him." He ruffled my hair as we walked by. Mary and I giggled, but no one knew why. The grand finale was a cold bottle of soda pop for each child. Selection could be made from strawberry, orange, grape, lemon, or cola. I could feel Linda's envy as all the others told me how lucky I was.

Even the boys gathered around me – even Tom Jennings! He had brown eyes, and I had a crush on him that year in third grade. Mother insisted on recording the class on film. My front tooth was still out, and I was surprised a golden jeweled crown didn't show on my head. My popularity was ensured at least that day!

Many years later, an assignment in my creative writing class in college was to compare ourselves to the main character in Haven Kimmel's book *A Girl Named Zippy*. I am going to share this with you because it gives great insight into my core personality and philosophy toward life. I haven't changed regarding my ability to make the ordinary day an exciting adventure. Here is my review of Kimmel's charming book:

A Girl Named Zippy is an enchanting book written for adults from a child's perspective. She was called Zippy because she was so active and energetic. Zippy grew up in the small town of Moorehead, Indiana. For over forty years, its population seemed to remain around 300, although not the same 300 people. Some were born, raised, and died there, but Zippy's family moved there from New York in the 1960s. There were no theaters, no department stores, or even a liquor store in Moorhead. Yet the little girl named Zippy tells about her very exciting and interesting childhood. This is mainly due to her colorful view of life and humorous way of linking words into a chain of events of fanciful observations.

She describes a collection of assorted scenes, almost like a scrapbook of her memoirs. These included, among others, the grumpy drugstore owner named Doc Holiday and the postman who only delivered mail to the people he liked. Zippy revealed the town's poverty and the cruelty of a teacher with such descriptive terms it opened up my childhood in Amarillo, TX, in that same era. My math teacher stood me at the blackboard, humiliating me in front of the whole class quite often.

Zippy's father was her champion, just like my dad was mine. His church was in the woods, and his sensitivity and adept insights influenced Zippy. My father lived his religion in another way until he died in 1994. Dad was a sincere Baptist who took me on morning walks and always suggested we pray on a park bench before returning home. I learned from him to respect all persons, no matter what color or creed. It seems both of our dads had compulsive behaviors. Zippy's book describes her father's unnecessary, elaborate preparation of the camper for weekend trips. My father drove everyone to distraction, putting string on a box to mail it, washing a dish forever, or sweeping in little squares. I loved my dad dearly but didn't see him often due to his addiction to work.

Zippy's mother was an absentee parent who spent a great deal of time in the closet looking for things and reading books. My mother was an accountant for Dad's business. She was at church a great deal, and we didn't do anything together except shop and eat. Zippy had her devout Quaker mother taking her to church all week long, and my grandmother insisted on long hours of family prayer nightly.

Getting a TV was a big deal because television wasn't available until I was 10 years old. I watched Flash Gordon and wanted to go to outer space like he did. I remember playing a lot of the same games that Zippy describes: jump rope, dress up, and jacks. Our families sang around the piano at night. I climbed a beloved cherry tree, just as Zippy spent time in her favorite oak tree. We both played in nature a lot and used our imaginations.

Zippy described staying up most of the night at slumber parties. She described her dream when she fell asleep at one of these parties. In her dream, a troll was sitting on the arm of the couch, running his ugly fingers through her hair. She woke up with a start, only to find the girls had gotten their cat Pee Dink to chew on her hair. I had a similar experience, dreaming of a rat biting my ear. What was happening was the pet hamster, Vanilla, had escaped from her cage and was building a nest in my hair as I slept. I had the vivid memory of jumping up, screaming, and running to wash pieces of paper and string from my hair at 4:00 a.m. that fateful morning.

Zippy also tells of being chased by a bull. My summers were spent at my cousin's farm out from McLean, Texas. We went for a walk along the creek bed that had mostly dried up. I had my shoes off, leisurely walking along and picking up rocks. All of a sudden, my cousin yelled as a bull charged toward us. We ran faster than I had ever done before or since. I dropped my shoes in flight and ran over the area of quicksand so fast that I didn't sink to my knees like I usually did. We headed across the cow pasture, over brambles and stickers that I didn't feel until later. Just as the bull lowered his head, gaining speed, we jumped over the fence, and he butted into the wood railing.

I can see a similarity between Zippy's unique concepts and mine. She found the most mundane things to be magical, just as I still do. She describes playing the card game of gin rummy with her Dad and deciding that certain cards were girls and some were boys. She made up her own rules and changed the whole game by refusing to take the boy cards her dad was dealing her. I have always made new rules and lived by my own standards rather than societies. It seemed nothing really big happened in Zippy's life, yet everything was important. Her philosophy was to value the small things and avoid focusing on the troublesome times. In this way, your mind takes a series of positive, random experiences and strings them together to make life a magical adventure. My whole life has been based on this same belief.

The Age of Innocence

The 50s were an era all to its own. I feel blessed to have been a teen in that period of history. It was the days gone by. The biggest offense for my friends and me in junior high was getting caught chewing bubblegum. Nothing big happened, but I felt everything was important.

We heard about the hippies and the beatniks out in California, but there weren't any in Amarillo. At least none that we knew or saw. Times change. Now, people with different preferences and values have turned from peaceful to violent protests. The year 2020 brought catastrophic changes to all the things I felt were true about America. I saw a level of discord and violence among genders, races, and religions. The definition of freedom I had counted on while growing up changed into a political fight. The 2022 Roe V. Wade Supreme Court decision reversed a fifty-year-old law regarding women's right to control pregnancy.

In the 50s and 60s, I felt safe and never thought about guns, mass killings, or hostages. I didn't have to worry about a mass murderer coming into our elementary school. These events were not in our reality or scope of reference. Now they're on the news daily everywhere. I don't know how the youth today face the challenges the world puts before them regarding violence, drugs, and sex. Violent computer games foster killing, and there's a general desensitization to inhuman behaviors.

I remember when the Cotillion Dance Club marked each season's change. Filling our dance card was a true sign of popularity. I got my first kiss from a boy at thirteen in the hallway of the country club where this event was held. Terry McEwin gave me a slobbery French kiss, and I thought I was going to die. I went to the girls' restroom with repressed, dry heaving, and quiet tears tumbling down my face. I was afraid I might have just gotten pregnant. The rest of the dance was a blur.

The next day, I talked to my sister-in-law. She was my confidant and twenty years my senior. I just told her I might be pregnant. I got no further in my story before she screamed, "Wait, wait, wait! We have to talk to Mother about this." Mother got involved, and I was called on the carpet!

When the tribunal of two convened, they asked what had happened. When I told them about the kiss and my resulting fears, they both looked amazed. With a disgusted look on her face, Mother said, "That's it? That's all?" I began to cry at her angry tone, tragically thinking, 'My life is over!' The conversation settled down into a lecture by Mother, which began something like this, "You never listen! Last year, when you had your 12th birthday, I gave you a book that told all about how babies get here."

I remembered the book *The Stork Didn't Bring You,* by Lois Pemberton (1948). It had cartoon sketches and was like my health book. I had lost interest and don't think I finished reading the whole thing. If you read between the lines, you would know less than you did before you began. It was so discreet that I missed the part about conception.

I hadn't asked questions about sex to prompt the book being given to me in the first place. I thought babies were a gift from heaven. I didn't even realize what my mother and sister-in-law were trying to tell me at thirteen. We never mentioned the subject again. Conception was a word I had to look up in the dictionary years later.

At least my mother told me there was no way I was pregnant. With a revolting, abhorrent look on her face, my sister-in-law added emphatically, "That was just a nasty, messy kiss, and you should never let a boy do that again!" I felt better that I wasn't having a baby, but I wanted a bath recalling the church's sermons about sins of the flesh.

17

It was all my fault that I let him kiss me. But how could I have stopped him? He just stole that kiss in the hallway next to the kitchen. He was twice my size. I guess I was a sinner and doomed. No one ever told me I wasn't. It was my first kiss, so I didn't know then how wonderful kissing can be when a couple shares loving intimacy.

That weekend, Mother gave me a quarter to go to the movie to get the whole incident off my mind. I went to see the musical *Seven Brides for Seven Brothers* for the sixth time. It was my favorite show, along with Debbie Reynolds and Howard Keel in *Annie Get Your Gun*. It was only going to cost 9 cents for my ticket because I didn't have to pay the adult price of 25 cents for those over sixteen. Mother gave me enough money to buy a soda pop and popcorn. She gave me an extra dime to call home if I needed help, as always. Seventy-five cents would cover any emergency in the mid-sixties. I always had to report where I was going and exactly when I would be home. Mother needed to know if I was going to be gone over a couple of hours. If we went to a movie, danced, or picnicked in Palo Dura Canyon, I had to get permission to be out longer.

That is why I mentioned the awful term 'coke date' to her. Soda pop was an important factor in my life. We never mentioned Coke or Pepsi in my home since Dad owned a competitor franchise. Mother would give me a lecture about loyalty if I told her I was going on a 'coke date.' As everyone knew in the '50s, a Coke date consisted of going out for a soda. If she only knew what a coke date means now! Coke is cocaine to everyone nowadays. My grandchildren told me that, to my surprise, many years later.

In the 1950s, teenagers would drag up and down Main Street between the two drive-ins which had hamburgers, sodas, and malts. You could go inside or stay in the car and have the carhops bring your order on roller skates. If you had a date, you'd go in and sip on an ice cream soda with two straws. It was fun to stay in your car so you could see who was cruising by in the carloads of yelling kids. We'd sit on the hoods of our cars, flirting and giggling. Nine-thirty was the curfew for me and all my friends.

I didn't want to stay out later, nor would I have been permitted. I don't know what the boys did after that. I never thought to ask. Yes, it was a refreshing time of poodle skirts, saddle oxfords, net petticoats, shopping, the jitterbug, and be-bop-a loo-la. Many years later, the 1978 movie *Grease* was an accurate depiction of our social culture in the 50s. It was my daughter's favorite movie as a young teenager, and her brother complained that she had watched it seventeen times.

My Spirituality

The first open dialog I remember with my Guardian Angels was at five years old. I used to see them as golden blurs of light filling my room. Jesus was often present to comfort me. I still have the same devotion as this child who fervently believes that God's Divine Light is directing my life. Jesus was and still is my connection to the celestial realms.

The Angels, nature spirits, animal totems, and gemstone guardians are also my friends. I was told all these companions were in my imagination throughout my childhood, I also had a special connection to the trees and the animal kingdom. I spent a lot of time as a child in a cherry tree in our backyard talking to a little red-breasted robin.

I played with the fairies in the park near my home. I saw their streaks of various colors weave their light as they flew from flower to flower and danced in the circle of trees. Sometimes, when I lay on the grass close by, they took me to a crystal realm. They told me this is where they recharged their vibrations with joyful energy. I am still permitted entrance. Anyone who holds lighthearted, pure intent is welcomed in this higher realm of the Divine presence to clear blocked energy, worry, and negativity.

By the time I was in my preteens, I could see black energy coming out of the mouths of people who weren't telling the truth. I knew when their words didn't match the energy that was in their thoughts and feelings. I got into trouble when I told them this.

I asked so many questions my Sunday school teacher said I was a blasphemous heretic. I didn't know what that was, but when I talked to Jesus at bedtime, he said to ignore them because they just didn't understand what he taught during his time on Earth. I was kicked out of the teen department for my sincere questioning. If Mother had not had so much pull as the Director, I would not have been allowed back into

Sunday School class. I began to learn to keep my mouth shut in church and elsewhere.

I believe that Jesus came to teach us about our capacity to create miracles through the power of unconditional love. I have studied the laws of karma and feel we all pay for the hurtful things we do to ourselves and others. Spiritual Law expresses caring concern for all individuals. The COVID pandemic reminded us all to take care of one another. Only by doing this can we stop the rapid spread of this virus and restore our economy.

Many people confused the preventative measures of mask-wearing and other safety restrictions with freedom of choice, political position, and religious practice. In the final analysis, all our actions affect every one of us, and we all pay the price for careless actions. It doesn't matter what our gender, color, or religion is. We all live on this planet and have a responsibility to care for all life. Violent protests are not the path to resolution.

CHAPTER TWO

MY PARENTS AND ME

I had to hide a lot of my lifestyle from my parents because it didn't fit their dreams for me. When I left the Southern Baptist Church at twenty-eight and joined the Unity Church, I never told them. When I went to a Chiropractor and became a vegetarian in my thirties, my half-brother gave me a stern lecture. I never mentioned my ideas on natural health to them.

My mother would have worried. I always tried to avoid worrying her, but she seemed to feel it was her duty as a good parent. One of my half-brothers used to call and yell at me in the middle of the night. He scolded, "Your crazy life is killing Mother!" Mother wanted to be a victim and loved to get my brother's pity by telling him how my life upset her. I kept getting married and divorced and moving, so I am sure it was distressing.

My Dad

My parents had a diverse upbringing. Mother was raised in affluence, and Dad in poverty. Dad had been raised on a farm near Erick, Okla. He was the youngest of thirteen children, and his father had died just before he was born. He was so proud of the penny he got under his plate on his birthday as a child. He talked about tough times but never really saw them that way.

Dad trapped different critters and sold the hides to help with groceries. He told tales of accidentally trapping a skunk on the way to the one-room school he attended. Dad laughed as he told of being sent home because of the smell. His mother wouldn't let him come in until he bathed in the horse trough.

He also did chores for the neighbors and was enterprising at a young age. He worked hard at a general store on the edge of town and was manager of it by the time he was nineteen. He owned small grocery stores and apartment houses when he met my mother in his late thirties in Clovis, New Mexico. Dad told the romantic story of meeting Mother when she came into his general store to buy ingredients to bake cookies for her boyfriend. "When this beautiful woman asked me for dates, I responded by saying, "I'm busy this Saturday night, but I could take you out next weekend." That was it for both of them. They found true love! They dated, married, and honeymooned a year later in Cloudcroft, New Mexico. They were together for nearly sixty years.

Dad died on June 11, 1994. He was one of the gentlest, most kindhearted men I have ever known. He never spanked me or even raised his voice to discipline me. I remember my father as a very spiritual man who had high principles and lived accordingly. He thought it was important to avoid cussing and yelling in anger. He was a man of few words, but what he did say was important. His word was his bond, and he was highly respected in the community. In our early morning walks and prayer sessions, Dad expressed gratitude for all the blessings that the Lord had given us. My spirituality is based on the integrity my dad exemplified.

Many of the employees at Dad's bottling plant worked there for the whole fifteen years he was in the cola business when we moved to Texas. He advanced the employees' money for extra expenses like a down payment on a home or their kids' college fund. He conducted almost all of his business on a handshake and lived the principles of trust, honesty, and faith.

Dad felt there was one right way to do things. Most of this was based on religious principles of sin. Some of this was his obsessive/compulsive tendencies toward perfection. My folks moved to Oklahoma my senior year when Dad sold the bottling plant. Dad had a couple of destructive beliefs and often stated, "All good things come to an end." He also said, "It is too good to be true." In my therapy many years later, I realized how deep this was buried in his programming and mine.

Even though I know my father loved me dearly, he spent little time with me. He was so preoccupied with work. Once, he took me to a professional wrestling match. He had been a wrestler in High School and argued that none of it was fake. Although we didn't go many places together except church, I know he was proud of his only daughter. After all, he displayed that terrible elephant head paperweight I made on his desk until he sold the bottling plant. I wonder where that prized procession is now.

Dad brought lighthearted wisdom to everyone he met. It certainly got Dad out of some tight places when angry comments would have made the situation worse. He was jovial but took things seriously, never negating something that was important to others.

Dad enjoyed the minutes life offered and listened respectfully to others. He always told me, "You only learn while you are listening, not while you are talking. That is why you have two ears and only one mouth." Dad used integrity in his communication. I hope I can live up to this. Mother reinforced this by telling me, "If you can't say something nice, then don't say anything at all. Beauty is as beauty does." They gave me these values to pass on to the generations of our family.

Dad was a patient listener to everyone he met in every walk of life. He didn't say a lot. He was a quiet man who observed life with an amusing zest for living. He never met a stranger and brightened the day of all he encountered. He always had a joke or a story about growing up with thirteen brothers and sisters. He said it is important to tell your family stories and to pass on your heritage to the youth.

Dad was active up to the age of ninety. He tarred the roof of the storage facility he managed at 88 years old. At the end of life, when his organs were shutting down, I was at the hospital in Dallas with several members of the family. Dad's belief in an afterlife was very real to him. He felt we paid for what we did on this Earth.

I was having breakfast with my son Eddie at a restaurant near the hospital on Dad's last morning. Suddenly, I felt an immense need to get back to Dad's room. I told Eddie we had to go and to let me out and then park the car. I didn't wait for the elevator and ran up the stairs to the third floor. Just as I got to his bedside, I saw him reach up toward the ceiling. I heard him tell Mother, "Oh honey, they have come for me. I've made it."

Dad took one last big breath and was gone. A few minutes later, it seemed Dad was standing beside us, giving Mother and me a reassuring hug from the etheric realm of heaven. He is still with me from the other side of the veil, giving reassurance and love during times of trouble and transition in my life.

Mother's last words to Dad right after he passed away

"It is a great morning, darling. The sun is shining; it is a beautiful day for you to go to heaven. Just take a long step and you'll be there. I can feel you are in a better place right now. I'll be all right, sweetheart,"

My Last Words to Dad: "There will be plenty for you to do in heaven, Dad."

I heard my dad say from the other side, "I want you to know I love you."

My Mother

Mother was in a nursing home for the last few months of her life after Dad died. Her cataracts greatly diminished her eyesight and her independence. She died in 1998, just before she was ninety-two. My Guardian Angel had appeared to me in a dream and said, "If you want to see your mother alive again, go to Dallas." I was living in Colorado Springs, but you don't ignore such a message. I went to Dallas the next day. It was the last day she was coherent before her stroke, which left her in a coma for a few weeks. I spent the next two weeks reviewing our relationship as I sat beside her hospital bed.

During my life, I had let Mother build a tower of her opinions right in the middle of my consciousness. I was looking at myself through her eyes. She needed me to be helpless and dependent on her. She never meant to undermine my self-worth. She just needed me to need her. Mother regularly told people, "Don't give it to Peggy Jo. She will mess it up." Mother never realized how this affected my level of confidence when she negated me. Her over-protective parenting made me feel inept.

I needed to control things because I felt out of control. Throughout my life, I have been the classic co-dependent. Mother lived in her stereotyping and victim patterns of co-dependency and control. Dad was good at staying happy no matter what happened. He didn't understand games and never played hers.

Mother had fond memories of growing up on a cotton farm near Hannibal, Missouri. She told of sleepwalking with a pillowcase over her shoulder. When asked where she was going on the staircase, she replied, "I'm going to pick cotton." I doubt she ever did because they hired farm workers to do this task. She said most of them were black, and they didn't have to pay them much because they got free housing and food.

Mother thought she wasn't prejudiced and didn't see skin color. I think she was, though. She said, "Black folks should have their good schools. It's okay for them to ride at the back of the bus." I never agreed with her opinions and the inequality. This was Texas in the 50s and 60s. Prejudice was all over the United States and still is in some people's minds. This erupted in the 'Black Lives Matter Protests' of 2020. I believe all lives matter.

I never heard Mother put someone down or criticize others except fat people. She was revolted by their obesity and quietly pointed fat strangers out in stores to me with contempt. I think she hated her own slightly puffy belly she got after my birth. I decided as a child that I would not be loved if I ever got fat. If I gained a couple of pounds, love would be shut off like a faucet. I worried about belly fat because she especially mentioned this part of people's bodies.

My late husband often offered to help me lose weight when I gained twenty pounds. Take my word for it: a woman will not feel this is helpful. After he passed away, I had a boyfriend comment that I was gaining weight. He said he couldn't be with a fat person. I freaked out that the five extra pounds on the scale showed. My worst fear was coming true. Love would be taken away from me if I got fat. He said I was overreacting. I think I was reacting to Mother's disgust of fat people. Many times, we aren't just reacting to the current situation. There may be deeper associations and repressed hurt.

After her death, I reconciled my relationship with Mother. Her sheltered, closed-minded opinions, her controlling games, her absorption with my weight and my life didn't seem so important. Mother was a powerful, brilliant woman who had graduated from college and was teaching school before she was twenty years old. Both her parents were college professors, very educated and religious. The years she was made to sit still in church all day left her less than devoted to religion. She described herself as a fidgety child. She said she believed in Jesus, but I knew she wouldn't have gone to church after she married if it weren't for Dad's sincere dedication to the Bible.

I finally came to peace with my mother, and I have always loved her dearly. She was one of my greatest challenges and one of my most profound teachers. Mother was the product of the times and of her environment. Her last words to me on her deathbed were, "Stay close to God; take care of yourself and remember that I love you." I felt her love for me throughout my life, and she is still helping me from the other side. I wrote the following excerpt in my journal to heal and reconcile our time together.

Mother's Legacy

I saw Mother today for the last time. Ninety-two years had passed by for her. Fifty-five have come and gone in my life. I look at the joys and tears. Words so tenderly spoken were meant to protect. These affected me as controlling and judgmental. Guilt that my birth ruined her health and diminished her looks filled the caverns within me. Her strength consumed mine. Yet, our relationship has freed my inner being. Her gift to me was beauty within and without. I inherited the grace of a Southern lady. As an adult, I became a female with old-fashioned values in, a liberated woman.

I reflected on the good times and all the valuable lessons she shared. I experienced a closure of our struggles and differences and felt at peace with our relationship. Closure is critical to move on when a relationship changes its form. I wrote this poem as I sat by her bedside on the last day that we had on this Earth plane together:

For the Last Time

I prayed. I cried.
I remembered. I forgot.
Releasing the grievances
I healed the need to prove and please.
Traveling to our core
The heart of shared love
Nothing matters anymore
Just this pure essence.
She let go of her agenda for me
I finally was myself with her
Unconditional love spanned the years from my birth to her death.
I closed the contract of my lineage with an Irish blessing,
Until we meet again.

I went to visit my son on the West Coast after Mother died. I went to the sacred tree cove on the dunes near Pismo Beach, where the forest meets the ocean. My grandchildren and I named this the Butterfly Beach because so many butterflies were in the trees there. I did a private closing ritual for the Mother's Life Celebration. At the end of my ritual, I placed my ear on the ground and asked for my mother's final message to me from the spirit world. She said, "Daughter, be yourself!"

She said what she couldn't say to me during her life. While I was growing up, I stated over and over, "I want to be me!" This always made Mother mad, and she would angrily reply, "What does that even mean?" I think now that she is on the other side, she understands how hard I tried to be my own person.

Mother always wanted me to be the replica of her. She didn't realize how this would negate my whole being. Now, she sees the truth from a higher perspective. I would have become extinct if I had lived her life choices instead of walking my own path. Living her dreams for me would have killed the essence of me and my ordained calling.

Mother was a wise woman that I highly respect. She and Dad certainly kept their love alive for sixty years. I would like to share some of the advice she gave me in 1981. I wish I could have applied this advice and worked out the conflicts I had in relationships with men. I kept these words of advice that Mother mailed me from several authors.

Frank Herbert Sweet wrote the classic poem "Before It Is Too Late." In this, he states, "If you have a message or a loving word to say, don't wait until you forget it, but whisper it today." Eleanor Roosevelt wisely said, "We live in the present, the future is unknown – Tomorrow is a mystery, today is all our own." I don't know who wrote the following poem Mother sent me from a daily paper:

Marriage is made of little things.

A tender smile, a small surprise, and a special look in a loved one's eyes.

Comfort given, interest shown,

Quiet moments spent alone –

Little things so small and sweet,

That's what makes a marriage complete.

I don't know the author of the following wisdom that Mother sent me, but it certainly applies to the covid catastrophe of 2020. "It is better to look ahead armed with wise words than to look back in regret. Life can change in an instant, and we may not have the opportunity to communicate in person any longer."

CHAPTER THREE

REALIZING MY PATTERNS WITH MEN

My parents provided a role model of stability in their marriage. It took many rocky years, tears, and failures to finally discover how to maintain my own identity in a relationship. I would like to have stayed married throughout life as my parents did, but it was not in my destiny. During one of my crying sessions in later years, my Guardian Angel told me, "*The relationships in your life are the fabric of multi-varied lessons that comprise the story of your enlightenment.*"

I was innocent at seventeen when I graduated from High School in Tulsa, OK. I married right after that. My first husband was an act of liberation that turned into a splash of cold water in my face at eighteen. My first marriage lasted only about one and a half years. I learned you can get hit for eating a peach or wearing a flower. He said I ate more than my share of food and was trying to look better than everyone else at church.

I met him during the summer after my junior year in high school. My parents and I were on vacation in Myrtle Beach, Mississippi. My niece and nephews were with us, and he told them about an electric baseball game he had in the trunk of his car. He asked my parents if he could give it to my nephews and invited us to breakfast the next morning. When Dad declined, my new suitor followed with an alternate suggestion that perhaps I could just go to breakfast with him. Remember, it was the 'Age of Innocence.' Nowadays, Dad would not let me go.

I received romantic letters and phone calls for months. We were engaged by the Christmas of my senior year. My parents had planned for me to go to college. When I told them that I was getting married instead, they said I had to go to night school to have a skill. I chose cosmetology so I could be a beautician. I liked fixing hair and worked at an exclusive salon a few years later.

I didn't worry about prestige but worried about what others thought of me. I had the memory of Mother regularly saying, "What will they think?" Eventually, I questioned, "Who are they? Why does their opinion of me matter?" In my naivety, I felt money and prestige did not matter. I couldn't imagine people arguing over money. I thought people ate beans and laughed about it. So what if people had big or little houses? I didn't realize ego and power struggles existed. The adage 'keeping up with the Joneses' seemed silly to me. Why would anyone care to waste their time doing that?

I believe a person is nice to be with or they aren't. This depended on the level of love he or she had awakened within. I still feel this way. I had little awareness of the economic ramifications of different classes. My first husband had buried resentment of people with money. I was raised in upper-middle-class, so I fit in that category. Although his family didn't have money, he was popular because he was the football captain. I've never felt money is a measure of a person's worth. I have come to realize it is convenient, though!

I was seventeen and had just graduated from high school when we married and moved to Calumet, Michigan. It was very different than the mid-west. We went dancing at pubs with Polish accordion bands. I loved dancing with the old miners sweeping around the floor to the lyrics from "Those Were the Days' by Mary Hopkins. My husband was in the military and was transferred that next spring. I was told that he was kissing a girl in the back alley while I was swirling around the dance floor to the polka. No wonder he didn't care! I decided to let it go since he denied it.

His next assignment was in Madison, Wisconsin. This shock was a rude awakening in life and certainly didn't match my sheltered upbringing. My husband insisted I got the crabs from the commode in the bathroom we shared with others on our 2nd-floor apartment. I found out later that this is not the way it is transmitted. Our life was filled with arguments. I remember running in the rain, thinking, 'Why does life have to be this terrible?' I decided it didn't have to be and left with my puppy, Dottie, after a few months.

I moved to Wichita Falls, Texas, with my folks after my first divorce. I met a handsome young man through the lady who called on us from the Welcome Wagon. My second marriage was based on a wonderful romantic courtship, and we married six months later. I fell in love with love! What I knew of him and his family in that short time of dating seemed perfect. He was what dreams are made from. He was all my mother had ever dreamed for me.

He grew up in Texas in the upper middle class. His family was in business in the mid-west as mine had been. He wined and dined me with poetry and wild car rides. I was showered with roses and moonlight walks. He had been a sailor. He loved racing cars and riding around with a group of friends, drinking beer. When I met him, he had settled down in his family's business.

Although the marriage lasted several years, the romance ended on our honeymoon with a car crash in Dallas, Texas. A drunk hit our vehicle, throwing me through the windshield and into the front seat floorboard. My face was sliced open several inches beside my eye and under my chin. My left ear was cut off. Luckily my new husband put it in a pail of ice at the scene of the accident and took it to the hospital. I saw a flash of light and realized my Guardian Angel was with me.

All I remember was this old man in farmer's overalls coming into the emergency room. The nurse said, "Oh good, the doctor is here. We can begin surgery." I thought, 'Oh, my God! I am done for if that's the best surgeon they could find!' Then I passed out. My ear was saved by this world-renowned plastic surgeon, who was called in from a weekend fishing trip to the emergency room. I didn't wake up for six weeks.

While I was in a coma, I entered the tunnel of luminous white light. I met with Ascended Masters regarding my purpose. They said I was not finished with my lessons on Earth, so I decided to come back to finish this life. I spent time healing in the spirit world with my energetic companions and fairy friends.

Weeks later, still in the hospital, I awakened to my sister-in-law cleaning blood out from under my fingernails. My head was half-shaved and wrapped in gauze. A cut ran down the length of my left cheek. My mouth was wired shut, and my front tooth was missing. My whole face was swollen and solid blue.

I was released from the hospital in head bandages. All this put a damper on the romance. Especially since I had a lower back injury which later resulted in a ruptured disc and surgery in my 5th lumbar. I had to learn to walk all over again. Most athletics, like water skiing, hiking in the woods, and sex, were ruled out for a while. I must have gotten pregnant on one of the two days of our honeymoon before the car accident. Months of morning sickness can also ruin the romance. Reconstructive plastic surgery and a new front tooth repaired my looks, but not our relationship.

Our son Brent was born nine months later. He was the fourth-generation firstborn male, so we had to carry on the tradition by giving him the first name Ernest. The family agreed I could pick the middle name. Growing up, he went by his middle name, Brent, but sometimes used his family name as an adult.

Our marriage took second priority to my husband's climb up the corporate ladder. He had golf, sports, his hunting dogs, and a traveling sales job to keep him busy. I had another son and my only daughter, Lisa. We named our second son James Robert after my dad and called him Jim Bob. When our family later moved to Hollywood, he went into the entertainment field and took the name Trevor James. I will use this name when referring to him instead of Jim Bob as I relate the story of our lives.

We lived in Oklahoma City until our second son was born. Then my husband bought his grandfather's business, and we settled in Wichita Falls, Texas. Tragedy seemed to follow our life together. Our business burned to the ground, and so did our marriage. This marked the beginning of the end. I watched as thirty-foot flames came from our downtown store on the 10:00 p.m. news. I frantically got my neighbor to watch our three children and raced to the scene only to find a do-not-cross tape. A policeman blocked me from getting any closer.

My husband was supposed to be at work, but they said no one had left. Thinking he must be dead, I went to my in-law's home in a daze, only to find he had been at the local pool hall through the whole evening. He saw the same 10:00 p.m. news report of the fire and called his parents to say he was okay. Our babysitter said I hadn't received a call that night even though she was watching our phone.

A year later, more distance was brought between us. He went back to traveling after the store burned down, and we moved to Ft. Smith, Arkansas. I often felt neglected. We planned for me and the children to meet him at the motel where he was staying that weekend. I arrived Friday about 6:30 p.m. with our three children under five years old.

Lisa was in a plastic infant carrier, and I brought her a playpen. My husband forgot we were coming and was out drinking until 11:00 p.m. The desk attendant would not let me in his room since he hadn't given permission. We weren't authorized by the person who rented the room. Since there were still no cell phones in the late 1960s, I sat in the lobby with the playpen, trying to entertain three sleepy children for nearly five hours. I had no money for snacks, much less for a room.

This was one of many times I was forgotten as our plans were put on the back burner. I told him, "I'm very unhappy." He replied, "That's ridiculous! We have a perfectly great marriage." It was not great for me! We couldn't communicate. I moved back to Dallas to keep up with his quickly advancing career. After a disappointing seven years of trying to get his attention, I filed for divorce.

I met the next important man in my life at Parents Without Partners in Dallas. My third husband was another vain attempt to find my knight in shining armor. We married and moved to Oklahoma City. He was going to college to get his prerequisites for Logan Chiropractic College. This required a move to St. Louis, Missouri. We had a wonderful son named Eddie during our five years of marriage. I learned to budget and provide for the family by doing some babysitting and teaching homeschool.

We couldn't afford preschool for Eddie and my three older children, Brent, Trevor (Jim Bob), and Lisa, so I started one in our home. The kids and I watched ants crawl, and caterpillars turn into butterflies. We pressed fall leaves, took field trips to waterfalls, and brought home water lilies from canoe rides. The neighbors asked if they could send their kids over because it looked like we were having so much fun. They gave me money when they were able. I advertised for other kids to join my home preschool. Since I didn't charge a set fee, I got all kinds of vegetables and various donations to help our family get through those tight times financially.

After the move to St. Louis, my husband only stayed in school for about a year. One Sunday morning, my third husband left without notice to remarry his ex-wife. He left me with four children, one dollar, a bag of beans, no car, and no job. I also had past due rent, phone, and utility bills. I soon discovered that I had shut-off notices and an eviction notice because he had been stashing money to leave for several months,

He left two days before Halloween, just after our son, Eddie, was one year old. I heard he was moving back to Dallas from our two friends after he went by to tell them goodbye. They said he told them he was going back to his first wife. I called her in Dallas, and she said they were getting remarried the next Tuesday. I told her she had better wait for me to get a divorce if she wanted it to be legal.

She sent him packing, and he came back banishing a gun on my porch a few days later. I bluffed my way out of his threats by saying, "Go ahead and shoot me. I will live to turn you in and haunt you in your jail cell forever." Of course, I would have died with the bullet he had pointed at my forehead. He left with a dazed look, and I went into shock for about twenty-four hours.

I had to get busy getting my life pulled back together. My half-brother called and offered for the kids and me to come to his home in Amarillo, TX. He said we could stay with him, his wife, and four children until we could get a fresh start. I declined, although I never forgot how inspiring this offer was to me. My other half-brother called at 2:00 a.m. and cussed me out for upsetting Mother again.

I had four part-time jobs within a week. I was a seamstress for Lane Bryant Ladies Ready-to-Wear, took in sewing and babysitting at home, and worked for a modeling agency. Sewing was hard because of my dyslexia. I made a lot of mistakes, ripped a lot of seams out, and started over. Yet, the garments looked great when I finished them.

The kids didn't miss any meals. I was able to keep our hundred-year-old, two-story home after all. I soon got a management job, which saved the day financially. I needed a balance of time in nature and recreation. I bought an old Wonder Bread truck, and we went camping most weekends. The kids and I painted cartoons on it and made the headlights into the eyes. She was a maze of artwork, so we named her

Mazie. The years the kids and I shared were a reprieve from the pain in my marriage. I treasure our time together through the years.

Growing up, I was programmed that I was supposed to get married, be a good wife and mother, and have a man take care of me. In the early 1960's, this program meant that a woman went to college only to find a good provider. That didn't work out too well for me. I didn't make it to college until after I was sixty years old.

I never seemed to make my mates happy, and I failed to get them to fulfill my needs. I finally learned you can only make yourself happy or unhappy. I asked myself, 'How many ill-rated relationships must I encounter before I stop this self-destructive cycle?' I was disappointed by most of the men in my life because they couldn't live up to the high standards my father had set. This was a hard act to follow.

It's no wonder I couldn't make marriage work. I had co-dependent concepts and fairytale illusions. In my marriages, our conversations eventually became limited to surface comments to avoid explosive arguments. Communication was like walking through a minefield. The result was superficial exchanges that lacked intimacy. I wrote this poem to summarize my attempts at romance and marriage:

Promises of Love

You say I love you,
But why should I endure
Communication comes less each day
As you find excuses to stay away
Others that you cherish hold their time-worn lure
Heavy-hearted, I cry for our bond
Pledged from feelings so fond
Trust broken, lies spoken
Fear abides, as pure love hides
Empty corners of the mind
Fill with images of demons I find.
Racing in circles of thought,
All is lost which I've sought.

The Merry-go-round

In my spiritual studies, I learned that a person must repeat a cycle until they have learned the lesson of this experience, and so we go around and around. The person must change the basic beliefs that created the problem and make different choices. I have had a pattern of choosing men who weren't available to me emotionally, physically, mentally, or spiritually. In one way or another, I kept myself continually abandoned. It took me almost seventy years to pinpoint this pattern. I guess I'm a slow learner. Emotions can take you around and around. A relationship beginning as friends can go in any direction. The tangled web of love took me on quite an unusual adventure. Life really can be a merry-go-round. Where did it begin, and where will it end?

When Eddie's dad left, our two best friends from Logan College were of great support to me. Their marriage was in trouble, and I didn't want to get in the middle of that. I told the man (my fourth husband-to-be) to call when they had worked things out, one way or another. About six months later, he called and said, "Good morning, I'm free." He was moving out and needed a place to live. I was still in the pattern of needing a man in my life. He moved in with me, and we were just friends. It didn't take long for us to take our relationship to the next level.

He was not over the guilt of leaving his marriage and two children. He went back and forth between me and his ex-wife, trying to justify his leaving. He wasn't really free, and neither was I. He moved out of my home. We talked, dated, reconciled, and he moved back a few months later. We married to resolve our confusion. Not too wise, right? I thought it would give me the upper hand over his ex-wife. Wrong again!

Our marriage ceremony was not a standard 'I do' ceremony. It involved personal commitments that we each wrote. The wedding took place in a beautiful spiritual setting in an exquisite garden called the Jewel Box in St. Louis. My best friend Melinda was my maid of honor. We all stood up together, but I stood alone a few months later in court.

Before I go on with that story, I could summarize our relationship by relating one encounter. It was my day for the carpool. Three neighborhood children flocked into the kitchen just as my three school-age kids and two-year-old toddler emerged from petting the kittens in the basement. They left the door open, and the tiny kittens ran pell-mell in every direction over the kitchen floor. The kids and I were all running every which way, trying to pick them up safely so we could get to school on time.

My husband, all dressed in white muslin, glided in the kitchen about then. With hands clasped and head raised upward, he quietly said, "If you were One with God, the kittens wouldn't bother you." This was the only time I ever destroyed property. I threw a cup of coffee at the wall next to him and gave him a dirty look. He left the coffee, broken glass, and the noisy bedlam for me to deal with. He glided back out the kitchen door, and we never discussed it again.

About six weeks later, I was conducting a seminar as a trainer for three hundred people. My new husband had stayed at his ex-wife's the night before. No, not again!!! I left my wedding ring on the kitchen table with a note for him to get out before I got home. He didn't have money as a Chiropractic student. The next thing that happened was totally unexpected, and the merry-go-round took another turn. My new husband moved in with my maid of honor. Yes, the one who was my best friend. His ex-wife wasn't ready to reconcile, and he needed a place to stay.

Melinda said they were just friends, but I knew where that idea had led him and me. My friend called a couple of weeks later and said she needed to talk. As the conversation developed, she said something about their fish. I thought, 'This is just great! He is still my husband legally, and she is talking about the aquarium in their apartment!" What about me?"

My mind flashed back to a few months earlier at our wedding in the beautiful garden setting, and now they were living the life we had planned. All my upbringing said this doesn't happen! I cried for two days, but it didn't change things. My life just didn't follow the Ozzie and Harriet example. I couldn't fit in that box.

All's well that ends well, they say. We all 'tried' to be spiritual over things. I told Melinda that I realized they were better suited than we were. I gave my so-called blessing. We had a meditation before she left that day. We visualized a still lake to represent our lives and released the situation into the calm waters. My ex-friend, ex-husband, and I turned over our lives to God's will. I haven't seen either of them since.

And what of me? I am reminded of Jean Lacordaire's quote, "All I know of tomorrow is that providence rises before the sun." I came to realize another meaningful excerpt I read at that time, "The past is a memory. The future is a mystery. Today is a gift. That's why it's called the present."

Something died in me that day, and something was born. Our marriage lasted less than fourteen months. We lived in the moment day by day. Yet, we couldn't connect these experiences to the ongoing time frame of the future. He returned a few weeks later when he and my friend broke up and wanted to reconcile. That was not going to happen. I had moved on. In reflection, I wrote this account of our ill-fated encounter:

Perceptions of Young Love

Said she, "Here I am. Can't I bathe you in loving kindness and fill all your needs?"

Said he, "Oh my love, too soon you come to me, for liberty and adventure await this young man's heart."

Said she, "I need your arms to need mine."

He replied, "Your love cripples me by demanding I remain unfulfilled without you. You need to feel valuable to one special person. I can give you this more completely when I am whole within myself."

He continued, "Set me free to find who I am. You are valuable to me even though I must search for myself. I cherish you as I bid you adieu."

Time passes.

"Good morning," said he. "I'm home." He returns just as if he hadn't walked away in a trail of her tears. "I found who I am; I want to end my search with you."

"Alas," said she, "You opened a door when you left that now becomes me; I must go on my quest with a free spirit. You would settle now, but not I. Each will do as we must." Then she left with a heartfelt sigh. Greater understanding comes with time. As the daisies begin to bloom in spring, forgiveness brings new opportunities into our lives.

So, you see, the adieu was the beginning. They part, each to find their own path as they move on to a new day. This offers a greater perception of mature love. I learned lessons regarding the extent to which two people can enhance one another. By each knowing who they are and accepting the other, love blooms. Through this budding, each finds the greatest gift of all: self-acknowledgment, for one cannot love another until self-love has been discovered. And what of young love? Alas, it comes too soon. Yet as life buds anew, true love shall come in another season!

My Lessons of Goodbye

I don't like parting. I've never been good at it
The flow – the come and go brings the passing of life's encounters
Their absence would not seem such a void
When I have a connection within
I'll create each moment's pleasure
From now on, I'll live for today
And let tomorrow come as it may

My Self-discoveries in Relationships

I journaled volumes of information over the years as I facilitated the healing of the struggles I encountered in life. My relationships guided my soul growth. These challenges supported my core beliefs about myself and motivated my need for change, growth, and self-love. I was in my late 30s, and the following circumstances had been a part of most of my relationships with men up to that time:

- I felt I was not competent and validated.
- I couldn't and wouldn't be heard.
- I was not the only sexual partner in my mate's life.
- I was not safe from angry outbursts.

Fear of failure due to past experiences guided my life choices. Guilt and embarrassment over my failed attempts to find true love ruled my life. Why couldn't I find my voice and realize I deserve someone who would be faithful and listen to me?

Patterns in Most of my Relationships with Men

- Extreme anger came at me out of nowhere, too intense for the incident that was occurring at the time.
- Abandonment – the rug was pulled out from under me in a shocking way
- Arguments escalated rapidly with explosive, hurtful words wielded at me
- I feel like I lived in a war zone with ambushes, land mines, and explosions
- Lack of stability and control
- Criticism of my size and monitoring of my food intake
- Lack of acknowledgment of the seriousness of our problems
- Not saying I'm sorry
- Lack of empathy
- Not being safe to discuss things to clear communication without a blow-up
- Being shut down if I voiced a complaint
- Not having my boundaries or my needs acknowledged
- Being hit out of nowhere for no reason

These were the type of individuals I chose for romance to discover my life lessons:

I had to heal these traits on deep levels of past experiences within myself as well:

Types of individuals who:

- Were not available, either mentally, emotionally, physically, or spiritually
- Cared more about other women or drugs than about me

- Were not listening to me and really didn't want me to talk
- Did not feel words were important and made broken promises
- Hid in game playing and lived in denial and rationalizations
- Didn't have the desire to grow spiritually, mentally, or psychologically
- Twisted their words around and said what was said had not happened
- Made a grandstand to discipline me for crossing them and disagreeing with them
- Were angry because they felt a loss of control by my mere presence in their life
- Ignored what was important to me
- Took the same stance over and over with no resolution made from my requests for change. (This resulted in lengthy talks and painful fights going nowhere.)
- Interrupted me and refused to see us in an equal partnership
- Criticized and tried to manipulate me continually
- Tried to control me with anger and fear tactics that didn't allow me to feel safe
- Used a dominating posture, asking loaded questions to pressure me into submission
- Treated me like a silly child without any business sense
- Thought I needed to be trained and harassed into obedience
- Were obsessed with maneuvering conversations to avoid losing a conflict
- Used anger and words as weapons to destroy what they couldn't control (basically, that was me)
- Wouldn't give me the time I requested to calm down and reclaim myself, my inner control, and my self-worth. This kept me off balance and out of my center.

An Exception to the Rule

My fourth husband was quiet and not abusive but was just not sure whom he wanted to be married to. Actually, three of my husbands didn't know how to be monogamous. My fifth husband and the father of my two youngest sons was not a part of these awful patterns. We grew apart raising the children, and our vows weren't enough to hold us together after thirteen years. My last husband, Dan has never done these disrespectful things. I finally found my chosen life mate after I found myself. I was in my 70s before I found my true love and life partner designated by the Divine.

Patterns of My Emotional Reaction in Relationships

In most of my relations with men, I had an obsession to be heard and to work out improved communication. I seemed to be stuck in egotistical interaction due to my insecurities.

The Consequences I Suffered by the time I was Sixty-five

I had post-traumatic stress. I also had chronic stress levels that created serious health problems for me, including a stroke, macular degeneration, high blood pressure, low blood sugar, and skin cancer. I had short mental whiteouts, during which time I had no thoughts or memory.

I had severe panic attacks that left me exhausted and depleted. I would shake and go into shock when these panic attacks hit me out of nowhere with severe pain. I felt like a saber was sticking through my back and piercing my heart as it extended out of my chest. I usually passed out when I had one of these anxiety attacks. Once, I hit my head on the tub in the bathroom when I passed out and fell. I was unconscious for an hour.

How I felt in Times of Conflict

Smothered and drowning
Emotionally unsafe, used, and disrespected
Threatened with extinction in the interactions of intimidation and diversion
Erased and crowded out of my existence in my own life
Ignored and forgotten
Drilled and cornered

What Home Was Like in These Times of Turmoil

Home was a place I wanted to leave to recover my peace and internal connection. I felt I was imposing my presence in someone else's home and not setting up our new life together. I lived in the chaos that we called home. I never felt safe from attack or abandonment, even when things were calm. Experience has shown me this was usually the calm before the storm.

We lived in a maze of confusion and misunderstanding that divided us into two opposing sides of a battle. If we could have put away the verbal slings, darts, and arrows and made a pact for peace, we could have built a safe place for intimacy. The things I didn't get to say became wrecking balls in my head. Fear-based thoughts and insecurities destroyed what might have been. I suffered a grave loss in these battles of will.

I had to heal my patterns of abandonment, severed trust, and lack of closure. I questioned, "How deep is the hurt, and how long am I willing to carry the wounds?" I lost my joy, spontaneity, and playfulness. I lost my creativity and ability to think straight. I lost myself, my purpose, and my will to live. My children were my refuge. I had to keep up appearances for their security. The traumas motivated my research to find peace of mind.

I had to straighten out my life drama and was frantic to clear my issues. Compulsive action kept me going on adrenalin. I had to learn to rest and to just stop before I dropped. Sometimes, doing nothing is just the thing to do. I once read, "It is not what happens to you that matters. It is the way you respond to it that makes the difference." I used to tell my kids, "It is not how many times you fall; it is how many times you get back up." Well, I am the comeback kid! Life goes on.

My guides once told me in meditation that my life was like a tapestry or a patchwork quilt. My relationships have been the vehicle of my growth. They make up the intricate patterns and brilliant colors that designate the path of learning for my soul's evolution. I chartered my course and lived my life my way, never sacrificing value or gain. I have been up and down the economic ladder, in and out of all cultures and class structures. I have had men from twenty-two to eighty-two in love with me – or so they thought. What most of them actually loved was my untamable, wild innocence. I go to the limit to live in all facets of work and play. I put my whole heart into loving. My challenge was to discover how to be myself and be in a relationship with another person. I managed to continue to raise my wonderful children despite my failure with men.

CHAPTER FOUR

LISA'S STORY

My daughter Lisa was diagnosed at Ohio University Medical Center at two years old as autistic. I was advised to commit her to an institution. I was a desperate, determined mother. I was not going to give up my child to the system or to the other world in which Lisa lived. I had a period of turmoil in my own life with a divorce. This resulted in great financial stress and many career challenges in the late 1960's. Yet, Lisa was my priority.

My search for a way to reach Lisa motivated my quest for the development of mental, physical, and spiritual healing methods. This led to the founding principles on which my teaching was based. I am going to regress in time to tell the miracle of Lisa's return to this physical plane from her place of retreat.

I couldn't accept the diagnosis that Lisa should be institutionalized. Yet, I realized something serious was going on with her. Attempts to get Lisa to talk during her first three years were impossible. At the time of the diagnosis, Lisa's behavior consisted of sitting on the floor rocking, humming, twirling a saucer, and tearing up newspapers to fill a plastic basket. She became very agitated and walked around fretfully on her toes until an empty basket with a stack of newspaper was placed beside her.

She filled a small round basket with the exact amount of paper she wanted. When she was content with the amount of torn paper in the basket, she lost interest, as if it didn't exist, until the next morning. If this activity was disrupted, she became extremely agitated. It seemed as if she was trying to collect her scattered thoughts and feelings into one container. In this way, she could know where they were. It was as though my daughter was functioning entirely by internal stimuli. She found her external environment overwhelming and frightening.

Lisa had withdrawn into a world of her own. Attempts of love and communication to her were not reciprocated. Her response didn't fit the stimulus. Often, there was no response at all. She didn't speak; instead, she shrieked and grunted when she wanted something.

At first, it seemed as if I was relating to a person who wasn't in her body. Her eyes were open but had a distant, unfocused gaze. She didn't look at what she was doing many times. At other times, she stared at something as if she were lost in it, and it was the only thing in existence. The first step was to pull Lisa's concentration from retreat to reality.

She had few facial expressions. She did not start talking until she was almost four. Her first words were a sentence, "I want water." She handed me an empty glass with a distant stare in her eyes as though she wasn't connected to the words. Lisa did not make full conversation until a few months later. It was a long road! Her brothers helped me.

When Lisa first began verbal interaction, she still had a blank wall expression on her face. Her brothers and I kept on sending love and talking as if we were talking to a normal child who was listening. We had thirty-minute listening practices and awareness activities three times daily. On a day of extreme withdrawal, this number would be doubled, but the time of each session would be shorter. I had her hearing tested as normal. I truly believe her attention span could be trained with effort and practice. Perhaps it was that 'knowing' and persistence that made it so. I believe we manifest with the focus of our thoughts and beliefs.

I frantically searched every avenue to reach Lisa. I sat for hours with her and learned to meditate to join in her world. I called in our Guardian Angels. They took me to a 'still point' at the apex of a pyramid. I was instructed to envision a flow of divine healing energy flowing through me and into Lisa. This was to be repeated three times over the next few days to bring this higher energy into manifestation magnetically.

The preschool I had at home helped with my income. I wanted to have time with my daughter and give her the opportunity to interact with other children. Lisa enjoyed being outside. We looked at tiny things in nature to stimulate her focus on the world around her. I have a love of nature, so we joined in this mutual interest. She seemed a little more responsive after times outside.

Lisa also liked to hear music with percussion rhythms and ancient chants. We used my Indian drum to make a repetitive beat. I made up puppet stories with virtues and values. Lisa was Timmy, the turtle who was learning to come out of his shell. She gradually began to come back to us and was speaking in full sentences. She didn't talk often, but I knew she could talk.

The principles in the book, *I'm OK You're OK,* by Thomas Anthony Harris (1969) helped teach Lisa and my other children respect and self-love. Harris used his views of Dr. Eric Berne's theory of (TA) Transactional Analysis. TA is a psychoanalytic theory used in therapy to understand behaviors and communication. It is based on three aspects of the whole person, including the parent, child, and adult. These concepts helped me discern if I was communicating from my analytical, judgmental parental aspect, the nurturing, supportive adult part of myself, or the childlike, fun-loving aspects of myself.

By understanding my motivation and how I was coming across, I could better understand the responses and behaviors I received. I also used Harris's concepts to build Lisa's self-image. Even though she seemed exceptionally bright, I knew she responded in different ways than the other children in our home and wouldn't interact. I thought if she felt better about herself, she might be more outgoing.

Children learn by imitating. I realized that Lisa's moods were a reflection of mine. I tried to practice the behaviors I wanted her to mimic. When I calmed myself with breathing and other relaxation techniques, her disposition improved. It was a strong stimulus to keep both of us from being nervous and overwrought. Lisa could be fidgety and agitated. She was calmer after our breathing practices.

As Lisa was able to join me in this practice for short periods, she became more expressive. Working with my daughter taught me to pace my schedule and my energy better to maintain equilibrium. I stopped rushing as much, but this was a continual challenge for me. My goal was to set a positive example of favorable behaviors that would bring a positive response.

By the time Lisa was eight, I had studied healthy diet principles. I tried this to see if it would help her brain transmit better signals in the mind/body connection. I decided to take the whole family off all processed foods. A natural diet made more sense to me. I got the book *Improving Your Child's Behavioral Chemistry* by Lendon Smith (1976). It deals with the blood sugar cycle and the removal of chemicals, preservatives, and processed foods.

I adapted our family's diet to include organic fresh foods grown in our garden with higher vitamin content. I watched closely for behavior changes to detect and eliminate certain foods. At the time I was experimenting with dietary factors, there was little published information to guide me, but by the turn of the century, scientific research began to support dietetic factors. Lisa had a food sensitivity to milk so she drank non-dairy substitutes like soy milk. A healthy diet free of chemical additives, preservatives, sugar, and processed foods was an important part of my daughter's recovery. I advise others to watch for this in dealing with autism and the inability to concentrate. Lisa began to come back to our world for longer periods as she stayed off these stimulants.

Years later, I read the book *The IQ Answer* by Frank Lawlis in 2006. His research shows there is a tendency in children with autism to have allergy responses that leave them susceptible to infections and compromised immune systems. Lawlis co-founded The Lawlis Peavey Psycho Neuro Plasticity (PNP) Center in Lewisville, TX. They provide objective diagnosis and treatment programs for individuals with neurological issues. These issues include autism, attention-deficient disorder (ADD), bipolar disorder, PTSD, and other brain-related problems.

Through the years, more studies have been done on autism. In 2009, authors J. McCarthy and J. Kartzinel's book, *Healing and Preventing Autism*, brought out a controversial theory that autism may be related to the increase in multi-vaccinations of infants. They also considered low glutathione as a factor in autism and suggested detoxification to clear the liver. Lisa had all the standard vaccinations required to go to school. In retrospect, I wondered if there was a connection.

Back to the struggle to bring Lisa into our world. Her brothers and I played games using deep breathing to help Lisa oxygenate her brain.

This helped her to be more alert and present in our activities. I was led by my Guardian Angel in meditation to follow a process of showing Lisa consistent unconditional love in conjunction with consistent structure.

Fortunately, Lisa was in the controlled environment of our home, and her brothers helped with this. This seemed to give her security to know what to depend on. The first few months after our lessons began, we took turns sitting beside Lisa, just being there and loving her. A key factor in bringing Lisa out of her sheltered world was maintaining our attention on her. Our love was there for her to reach out and touch whenever she decided to attempt this.

I had to accept there was a situation of severe emotional disturbance, but I was counseled by my Guardian Angel to concentrate on solutions. Words are powerful and can become a self-fulfilling prophecy. If you accept a label, you can be limited by this. Then you are unable to go beyond that expectation. We did not compare her actions with anyone else's. We used Lisa as her own yardstick. Lisa's brothers and I treated her as a normal child, and she gradually started acting like one.

I set my alarm to awaken early in the morning and spend time each day visualizing Lisa as happy, outgoing, and communicative. I journeyed to the place where she had withdrawn. I shared that place of retreat with her and was instructed by my Guardian Angel that she would return when she was ready to integrate fully into this world. I just allowed the energy of unconditional love to flow from my heart to hers and sent her mental messages that I loved her and hoped she would decide to join me and her brothers in life on the physical plane. A steady flow of love was directed to Lisa, encouraging her to share her awareness with us.

As Lisa came out of her retreat over a period of three years, she needed positive reinforcement by experiencing success. We encouraged her to begin to think for herself and praised her efforts to make small decisions to build her self-confidence. We incorporated physical activities such as running, jumping, marching, and hopping on one foot and then the other to develop large muscle control. She needed the movement since she had been inactive for so long. We played jacks, picked up sticks, and drew for fine motor control. She needed structure and a daily routine with little variance.

Lisa learned the ability to concentrate with listening exercises. She repeated a short rhyme after me. Praise was an important encouragement. We listened together for certain sounds in nature, such as the wind, rain, or a bird. Subtle nature sounds encouraged her to pay attention to the immediate environment and listen intently. After her verbal skills were demonstrated, I gave her creative thinking activities to describe a picture or scene in her own words to develop her right-brain, as well as her left-brain logic.

Lisa always demonstrated high intelligence. She could retain long phrases and repeat them. She loved to get stars on her reward chart. I used a form of behavior modification: good action equals good reaction; disruptive action equals loss of some privilege or treat. This gave her the ability to relate cause and effect by meeting her action with an equal reaction. This structure became the mirror reflecting the intensity of her actions. By watching our reaction, she learned the proper action.

Lisa went through a period of being very destructive with her own things. She always left the other family members' property alone, though. When she tore up her clothes, I put her nice things up. This taught her to take care of her things or to lose them briefly. When she drew on her toys with markers, paint, or crayons, she lost them for a while until she was given another opportunity to respect their intended use for play.

Lisa had no concept of time, so I didn't wait more than a twenty-four-hour period to present another learning opportunity. This removal of the crayons and toys would be done with a statement such as, "I'm sorry the crayons and this toy have to be put up. We'll try again soon to see if you've learned to write on paper." I realized this had to be stated in a matter-of-fact, logical manner from my left brain rather than emotionally admonishing her.

Emotions excited her into orbit. Lisa withdrew from the intensity of emotional energy. This taught me to control my frustration and avoid pushing for a specific outcome. We went over the same lessons and concepts. In the beginning, I had to set the guidelines and work toward a situation in which she had the maturity to impose the boundaries upon herself. The same is true when raising any child. It just required more structure and patience with Lisa.

Sometimes, a walk, a story, or music time would bring her back to our world to interact. For the longest time, she had no concept of interaction. She only came to the edge of communication but didn't venture forth. She chose unmatched clothes for school. Finally, I limited her choices and bought only things that could all be mix-matched. In this way, I created a situation of providing several correct choices.

On days of her withdrawal, I would plan special activities I knew she enjoyed. For example, I would use reverse psychology and announce, "I guess Lisa doesn't want to go with us to get a treat. I don't know why she wants to stay home with the sitter." Then, when the sitter arrived, her brothers and I gave her a goodbye kiss and left. Follow-through and consistency were of paramount importance.

Above all, I stressed that Lisa had to pull herself together and function in this world by her own choice. She had to make the intention and effort to reach out to us. She had to want to come into the physical plane with us. At the point she made this decision, we had rapid progress. She developed a sense of responsibility for her own actions and the consequences. This responsibility had guidelines that required her to feel proud of her accomplishment and realize her self-worth.

As the years rolled on, training in self-discipline was administered impartially to the whole family. When Lisa didn't pick up something of hers, it would go into the 'Saturday Box' along with the things her brothers left strung around. A processing fee of ten cents was applied to each item before they could get it returned. They were given their full allowance but had to pay me back the dimes owed. It seemed important for them to get their allowance and pay for the item out of this. If I found a pair of shoes, I'd say, "Your shoes are in the line of traffic. If I pick them up, they will go in the Saturday Box." They always had a choice to pick their things up or lose them until the next Saturday and pay a dime per item.

At the end of the week, if there were only three items in the Saturday Box, they would still have to pay thirty cents. They would get a reward on their personal Star Chart to encourage improvement. As the children got older, they were affected by the cost of living conditions. Items in the Saturday Box cost fifteen cents to retrieve, but their allowance also went up to five dollars per week in middle school.

Keep in mind this was in the early 1970s, and $5.00 went further. Each child had a small list of chores and would receive a star if these were done correctly in the required time frame with a positive attitude. I wanted to provide a glimpse of the adult world in an environment of simulated employment and the consequences of action. I knew my children would need good work habits and self-discipline as they got out on their own. I found a combination of firm discipline and reward was most successful. Consistency is the key to any training model.

Discipline was not confused with punishment or an angry attack on self-worth. There is a fine line of distinction between rejecting a child and rejecting their actions. When I had to correct any of the children, I stated, "I love you, but I do not like the way you are acting right now." My children began to work with me to correct the behavioral pattern that didn't give them positive feedback. This helped build constructive habits and self-esteem.

There was no difference in the code of acceptable conduct expected for Lisa than for her brothers. It just took longer to reach her with the training and simpler chores. Reward and loving consistency were the keys to accomplishing the best results. Of course, Lisa needed more structure and monitoring in her tasks with great loving approval for small progress. If Lisa did a sloppy job, the work was not criticized, but she was asked to try again. Then I'd show her what part was done sufficiently and specifically where improvement was needed.

I dealt honestly with Lisa. If she did a good job, I would tell her with genuine congratulations. We immediately put a star on the Star Chart. If she needed improvement, I would say something like, "That is almost right, but I think you can do better." The standard of expectation increased with her ability to comprehend and respond. She liked getting an immediate star. I set up a 'reward box' of items we called the Goodie Box.

Stars were rewarded for positive behaviors with rewards that the children could select at the end of the week from the Goodie Box. We went shopping at the Dollar Store, and each child got to pick things to be earned with star awards to put in the Goodie Box. Every week, I explained the reward connection again and held the Star Chart up to the Goodie Box. It took Lisa a while to associate the Star Chart and the Goodie Box reward.

I had not been taught to do chores while I was growing up. My mother sheltered me from work. She didn't seem to realize I needed to learn this responsibility when I was young. She thought I'd have plenty of time to work later in life. I don't think she wanted to mess with training me. All my children had minimal chores by the time they were five years old.

As they got older, I told them that a boss wouldn't let them keep a job as an adult for sloppy work and complaining. Bosses don't tolerate a situation of being ignored. They won't keep reminding an employee to do the work they are hired and being paid to do. The world doesn't work that way. I refused to let my children turn me into a nagging parent; I let them pay the consequences of their own choices.

One of Lisa's training priorities was to listen better and to follow directions. I made listening a pleasant experience by talking in a kind tone of voice. We had listening contests. As our lessons progressed, Lisa's favorite class was our storytime. When we first started the listening games, Lisa sat staring blankly throughout the whole encounter. I continued talking as if she were participating. As her attention span increased, so did my level of expectation.

In time, I got quiet when her eyes glazed over, and I knew she was off somewhere when I was reading to her. Finally, she reached a point of intermittent attention. The silence brought her back, and she looked at me questioningly. By this time, she was involved in interactions enough that she noticed I wasn't talking.

I acknowledged this by saying something like, "I didn't want you to miss this good part of the story, so I waited until you were listening." I sometimes replied in a calm, matter-of-fact tone, "I was quiet because I don't like to talk when you aren't listening." We kept up this pattern with many stops and starts. At first, we didn't get a single story finished before her ability to stay with it ended. She was either completely focused or fidgety and unable to sit still at all. We would try another time when she could focus. Eventually, as time went by, she would catch herself not listening and say, "I missed that part. Go back and read it again." She became motivated to monitor her attention span and increase it internally.

As the years went on, Lisa said that I didn't listen to her at times. I realized I had a pattern of withdrawal that went back to my childhood. I am referring to the mental cave I created that was quiet and safe from nagging and criticism. Lisa and I made up a game of listening, and each tried to return to the present time frame to be more consciously alert and attentive. We called it the 'Be Here Now Game'. We both had to work on this skill.

I didn't want my children affected by my moods. I didn't want them to be driven to perfection patterns to experience their worth or find daily equilibrium. As a child, I felt if I could only be perfect enough, I could avoid my mother's anger and silent withdrawal. I also thought if I performed well enough, I would be loved and noticed.

I felt it was important for my children to understand they did not have to earn love and attention. This was given unconditionally, and an environment was provided for each member to give acceptance and self-love to themselves. I wanted my children to experience consistency, integrity, and order in their environment.

Lisa had a short attention span. When she first returned to reality from her withdrawal, the main challenges were concentration, cognitive reasoning, and follow-through. I worked toward the point where Lisa would begin to endeavor to be a part of our family activities. Then my external structure of discipline could be replaced by her self-discipline. Lisa made great progress by the time she was five years old. Although she had many challenges, she attended public kindergarten,

Since Lisa needed excessive guidelines and consistency, spanking was not even a consideration. Any kind of harsh reprimand or physical contact only made her more defiant and distant. I developed a three-step system:

1. Ask her to complete something that I wanted her to do.
2. Remind her once.
3. Follow through with an appropriate mild consequence for ignoring me.

By getting directly in front of her and gently touching her shoulders, I made certain I had her attention. It was about two years before she would give eye contact and seem to be present in her body. She usually looked off with a glazed stare. Lisa was a part of our structured family. We had rules and guidelines to teach maturity and responsible behaviors.

My daughter was in second grade at elementary school when our family moved to St. Louis, Missouri. During the transfer, her records were lost. What a twist of positive intercession to avoid Lisa being classified as learning disabled or autistic. The new teacher asked if I had noticed she was distant at times. If this was all they recognized as different in her behavior, Lisa had a chance to be considered normal. She had made great progress!

Lisa attended public school, but in addition to this, her homeschooling included right and left-brain skills. I realized the importance of whole brain function. We worked on right-brain skills of creativity in art with crafts and drawing and performed original puppet plays.

Here is an example of our interaction to develop her left-brain reasoning and problem-solving skills. I asked Lisa to get a book from the shelf. She went over, but she came back empty-handed and just stood there, not knowing what to do. I saw the book on the shelf below the place she had been searching. I asked her if she looked thoroughly. She replied, "Yes." This was true, for she had looked in the same wrong place for a while. I asked her to look again. She looked in the same place and came back, claiming it wasn't there. I encouraged her to think of other places it might be. She looked pensive and stood in silence until a smile crossed her face. She went back to the bookcase and retrieved the book from the shelf below, returning with a look of triumph.

I praised her accomplishment. She completed the thought process of problem-solving with only slight direction and guidance from me. It was a breakthrough for us. If children are sheltered from thinking for themselves, their learning process is thwarted. It was easier to do things for Lisa, but she would not learn with the process of me doing the task or by me thinking for her.

It took so much repetition to get her involved, but the reward of her independence and pride of accomplishment was worth it. I found the struggle to try, fail, and try again was a necessary part of her learning. She progressed through small baby steps of success. Her maturity level was directly proportionate to her acceptance of responsibility. This is true with all children.

I took in sewing and home tutoring and didn't work outside of our home often until Lisa was in school. Then, I began a private practice tutoring in addition to a career in sales management. A lady who designed the 'Me Doll' contacted me from an article in the daily St. Louis paper on my success with emotionally disturbed and learning-disabled children. I purchased a doll that was personally designed to look like Lisa's. She equated it with the doll because it had yellow yarn braided hair and her favorite color of clothes with a mirror face. When she looked at the doll, she saw herself reflected.

One day, Lisa took a key and scratched the back of the mirror, partially taking off the coating. She couldn't see her whole reflection, and it made her face appear distorted. I asked her why she had done this. She said, "I was mad at myself, and I didn't want to look at me." She had attacked it as she did herself and her own things.

We talked about the way Lisa felt and watched the expressions on the mirror reflected in the doll. Lisa began to treat the doll with affection as her self-love increased. Her regimented training lasted almost five more years in our home classes. I arrived at the conclusion: A child is unique! A problem is unique! The solution must be unique!

Anatole France once stated, "The whole art of teaching is only the art of awakening the curiosity of young minds to satisfy that curiosity afterward."

Can we not also apply this concept to the learning and emotionally disturbed individual? He or she is a person to be taught, not a problem to be solved. The solution comes in finding the unique means and tempo. If a disturbed child is believed to have an incurable mental illness, this limitation can create this reality. If a child is treated as a problem, perhaps he/she cannot rise above the label of our expectations. If a child has trouble comprehending, it requires more patient training and persistence.

I taught Lisa and all my children to define their own measurements of success and set their own goals. I wanted them to love themselves and know they are lovable regardless of their accomplishments. I hoped they would avoid destructive relationships of abuse. I hoped that each would be unique. As they have grown through the years, I feel they have accomplished what I fostered.

We are all uniquely different, good friends who respect these differences and love one another for who we are. The ultimate purpose of a parent's love and training is to make dependency unnecessary. I vowed I would help all my children stand on their own. A parent's role is one of teaching independence, fostering self-worth, and providing protection. All my children have a profound level of maturity, emotional stability, and mental acuity.

Lisa's mind is exceptional, with a photographic memory. Many autistic individuals are savants. She was a cheerleader in middle school and on the honor roll. She forged her own way in life, graduating from high school at sixteen. Adult life came early at eighteen with many challenges for Lisa. She left college to raise her young son Cory alone. She raised him and excelled in several career fields as a travel agent, territory manager, administrative assistant, waitress, sales representative, customer service agent, dealer in a casino, and city tour guide. I am extremely proud of the adult Lisa has become. She has a great depth of understanding of herself and others. Her right-brain creativity is expressed in her exceptional art and writing abilities.

Here, in her own words at age twenty, is the account of Lisa's retreat within:

How do you write about something you don't understand or a time of your life you can't remember? All I could do was try to explain my feelings. I've blacked out a lot of my childhood. Maybe there are things too painful or scary to remember. Perhaps it was both. I do remember what it felt like to be in the little world all my own.

Thinking about it makes me want to cry, but it also gives me a feeling of peace. In that place, my place, no one could hurt or reject me, but at the same time, no one could love me either. The closest scenario I can give is being alone inside an old brick castle on an overcast, drizzly day. It is beautiful in a sad, lonely way but very peaceful.

I wasn't aware of what was going on around me a lot of the time. There was one time I do remember, though. I was sitting in a corner and tearing up paper into little pieces. I used to fill a small laundry basket a day. I was aware that someone was talking to me, but the voices seemed so far away. It took me a long time to comprehend what they were saying. My mother was asking me to go get some ice cream with them. I remember really wanting to go, wanting to be a part of it, but I was scared. I felt like no matter how hard I had tried, I couldn't have moved. It didn't feel like my mind was in sequence with the rest of my body.

It's a scary feeling hanging in limbo, just drifting and drifting, not aware of what is going on around you and not caring. Even the loneliness becomes less and less evident. It's like locking all your feelings up in Pandora's box. You know they are there; you just can't get to them. You're emotionless, existing without living. I don't remember any other incidences of that time in my life. I came out of it slowly with a lot of love and patience on my family's part.

I wasn't non-existent or non-reachable anymore, but I still wasn't relating to reality like other people. I would drift in and out. People would talk to me or ask me a question and I wasn't even aware of them being in the same room. I could tune out the rest of the world at the drop of a hat. I still find myself doing it now when I don't want to hear something or when I'm concentrating.

I was despondent and withdrawn during that time of my life. I became very rebellious. I refused to match my clothes. It's a trivial matter, but I don't know how many times my mother sent me back upstairs to change before school. It would make me so mad because I thought I looked fine and that she was just picking on me. I cut holes in my clothes and destroyed my room and my processions.

My mother took my special things out of my bedroom, and I only had worn-out clothes. I remember Mother saying I couldn't have nice things until I learned to appreciate them. I remember sitting on my bed and screaming. I felt like a caged animal who was not sure of its surroundings – ready to fight anything that got in its way.

I guess I wasn't sure of my environment. I was trying to adjust to a world that was totally different from the one I had been living in while withdrawn. The rest is a blank. A part of me wants to remember to understand. Another part just wants to let sleeping dogs lie. I'm still living between two different worlds. Sometimes, it's hard to see where I fit in. When the pressures, money, and loneliness get to me, I can feel that place. It's distant, but I know it's there. Someday I'm afraid I'll wake up and find myself there. Anything – even the loneliness is better than the emptiness.

One Smile at a Time

In 2018, Lisa came to visit me on her way to Alaska. She reached a point where she had to make a change to find quality of life. For her, this meant camping for five months in Alaska, zip lining, a helicopter ride, and hiking in the glaciers, among other adventures on her Bucket List. She left her job as a dealer at the casino, gave away almost all her belongings, and off she went without a return ticket. While working as a booking agent at a resort, Lisa *found* herself and discovered a greater meaning in life. Lisa's thirty-year-old son Cory said, "It was the first time I saw her living her life for herself. It made me proud."

After her tour job tour ended in Alaska, she went to visit each of her five brothers in different states around the USA. She called this experience a journey into her brother's life. She had a few days in each location to be totally in the moment and savor the relationships with each family member. Before going on to her next job assignment in a Colorado ski resort for the winter, she re-evaluated her priorities and concept of necessities vs. conveniences.

On the way to the airport to see her youngest brother, Lisa got quite philosophical. She said," I have never felt I would be someone of great fame. I feel my mission in life is to just touch people's lives 'one smile at a time.' She repeated the phrase 'one smile at a time, one smile at a time.' This insight made such an impression on me. I feel it is a gift that any of us can strive to share. Lisa truly lives up to her nickname, 'sunshine,' and brings uplifting light into the world wherever she is. After her visit with Patrick and his wife Anne, her younger brother commented, "She is the same person she's always been, but the long-awaited blossoming of her free spirit is refreshing. I'm watching and feeling warm and happy about this new beginning in her life."

CHAPTER FIVE

REACHING IN – REACHING OUT

This is the story of reaching out to my children and then sharing these findings with others. I just didn't accept that a way to help a child could not be found. I got insights when I prayed for solutions. I later founded my own company from all the work I did with perceptually disturbed children called Creative Learning Programs.

I attended a Unity Church in St. Louis, Missouri, and taught a three-year-old class. One of the women in the congregation was a personnel agent who placed people in jobs. She said my life experience had prepared me to be able to handle stress and multi-task. Raising my tribe of four children required organization skills and tenacity. In her estimation, I was management material, and she secured me an interview with Xerox Corporation for a job in their Education Division. I felt this was the Divine guiding me.

There was a room full of applicants in the initial screening. I was up against some stiff competition, and I had to put my best foot forward. I needed to get calm and centered, so I did what I had done as a child in a testing situation. I imagined I was in a spacecraft going up into the dark void. It was peaceful and quiet there. I wasn't stressed. Then I could think clearly. My Guardian Angel gave the answers to me.

I got the job after five interviews. In my final interview, the sales director tossed a stapler in my lap. He said, "This is an electric stapler. Sell it to me." There was no such thing as an electric stapler in the early 1970's, but the right words to convince him to buy it popped into my head. My Guardian Angel came through! The interviewer asked me to give him one word that best described me. I answered, "Perseverance."

I was one of the first women hired nationally with Xerox in sales management. I found out later that two hundred women had been interviewed throughout all the company's branches. I had the title Education Specialist because they gave me the school market. This territory had financial constraints, but I made 30% over my incentive target while I was in their employment. I also developed a program to use Xerox copiers for reproducing school curricula and communication in the Board of Education offices. My career was launched, and I was financially independent without a man to take care of me.

I had success in corporate America but never fit in there. After a few years, I left to start my own company in family dynamics and education. I discovered I could take care of not only myself but also my four children. I did it without any child support from my ex-husbands. Even though I didn't have a college degree in the 1970s, I was teaching color/sound vibrational benefits and breathing control in workshops for St. Louis schools. It was a time of innovation and confusion. They were taking the flag and God out of the school systems. The practice of Yoga was still associated with the devil.

I taught continuing education programs at all levels of public and private schools, from kindergarten to college. I was interviewed on the radio show Profiles in Education in St. Louis and was invited to be a regular on *Sesame Street* with Dr. Loretta Long soon after that. I decided I would not like big city life in New York, but my life was on an upward turn in my chosen field of family dynamics and child education.

More Challenges at Home

I had other challenges with my family. During my daughter's first few years in school, she matured slowly on a social level. I encouraged her to join in classroom activities and to speak up. I had another problem. My oldest son was having difficulty learning to read, so I developed a reading program to help him. He needed to see the whole picture to get the details. He was lost in all the rules and variances of meanings and sounds. My third son had an early-onset speech impediment.

I set up a screening series to determine exactly what a child needs to fill in learning gaps to reach their creative potential. I presented structured rules in sequential order and broke the reading process into small steps with phonics and phonograms. Each lesson was based on success at the child's level of accomplishment.

I called this reading program 'Creative Approach to Learning.' My son began by learning letter sounds with funny picture associations. We made a game out of combining different consonants and pictures. I continued to read everything I could find to reach my daughter and my two sons, whose brains worked in special ways. Together, time and a healthy organic diet were integral parts of my family's lifestyle. Lisa's recovery from being withdrawn and my two son's improved reading and speech were my motivation. I also saw improvement in my dyslexia and in my daughter's perceptional and directional difficulties.

I used Spalding's concept of grouping letter sounds in phonograms. In this process, several letters make one sound and are used in many different words. This simplifies the process of sounding letters with phonics. Through small successes, it gave my son the confidence to try the next step in a relaxed environment. His self-image and confidence level began to improve.

I also used *Psycho-Cybernetics* by Maxwell Maltz (1960). He discovered the science of cybernetics. It serves as a guidance system to steer a person automatically in the right direction to achieve certain goals. It also serves as an 'electronic brain' that can function to solve problems, give needed answers, and provide inspiration.

Maltz's theory is that the mind can't tell the difference between a detailed imaginary event and a real experience. His research proved that practicing in one's thoughts can improve performance in one's actions. My son was using this process against himself in the patterns of fear of failure and worry. We applied the principles in psycho-cybernetics to set a target goal and imagined it already in existence. You simply focus on the outcome and the goal that you desire.

Maltz warns not to be afraid of making mistakes since learning is accomplished by trial and error and remembering the successful patterns so they can be imitated. According to his theory, belief is the key. Our belief about what happens is more impactful than what actually happens. According to Maltz, the power of the mind to override events with one's attitude is amazing and produces a hypnotic effect.

The key is to make autosuggestions and then trust your creative mechanism to work so you will not use too much conscious effort. Relaxation is necessary to reprogram the old habits and beliefs so they can be replaced by new, more productive ones.

I didn't know the science of these techniques in the early 1970's. Yet, I was led by my intuition to apply similar concepts to aid better whole brain function. When I was working with my young son, I told Brent to visualize himself reading effortlessly and smoothly, recognizing all the words. I found if he tried too hard, he froze up in a fear of performance syndrome. Instead, he imagined the outcome he wanted. This initiated the internal process of bringing his goal into a successful actuality.

I told Brent that if his mind was going off course, he could make it self-correct over and over. If he held the chosen outcome he wanted in his concentration, he could eventually get his chosen result. Birds and other animals have an internal guidance system to find their way home or to another chosen location. Connecting to nature enables a person to establish a bond with one's instincts of inner guidance. Brent pretended he was like the birds who have a natural guidance system. He imagined that his brain could take him where he needed to go to reach his goal.

The book *TA for Tots* by Alyn Freed, Ph.D. (1974) helped build Brent's confidence. All my children enjoyed the stories that teach the transactional analysis concept of self-respect and self-care. Brent had much better success when he was positive. His memory even seemed to be better when he was in a good mood. The energy of destructive thoughts and emotions is a lower vibrational field of activity.

The Russian psychologist K. Kekcheyev tested people when they were thinking pleasant and unpleasant thoughts. He found that when people were thinking pleasant thoughts, they could see, taste, smell, and hear better and detect finer differences in touch. It was also found that memory is greatly improved. The mind is also relaxed when the person is thinking pleasant thoughts.

I made up adventure stories for my children with helpful feelings called sprinklets. These magical characters make you feel like fairy dust is sprinkled all over. Joyful, loving, peaceful, kindness, honesty, hopeful and grateful sprinklets are depicted as stars with delightful faces. Harmful emotions like fear, anger, guilt, worry, dishonesty, grief, sadness, loneliness, insecurity, and depression are pests that get in the way of happiness. I named these pestlets. Each one of us can choose to share sprinklets and live in harmony, but sometimes a pestlet mood takes over and affects others around us. I later published these in a set of six books entitled *The Healing Feeling Series.*

We are affected by suggestions and input from others. This theory of neuro-reprogramming is also enhanced in a process called *tapping, which* I learned many years later in my recovery process. Gary Craig's book *The EFT Manual* (1995) is now called the Gold Standard. The 'Emotional Freedom Technique' is extremely helpful in restoring balance when emotional traumas disrupt the body's energy system. Body meridians are reprogrammed to provide another response to past experiences by tapping on specific neuropathways and acupuncture points with the fingertips.

Brent moved very rapidly through the reading program. When I used it with other children, I always moved at the pace of their individual success level. The pacing was critical to ensure the child did not get bored, discouraged, or become overwhelmed. Reduction of stress and absence of fear were key factors in the success of the program.

My son Eddie, who had a speech impediment, also had left/right reversals. I used Edward DeBono's left/right marching and crawling practice sessions to help his neurological signals cross the midline in his brain. DeBono's book *5 Day Thinking Course* (1967) helped me with my dyslexia because we did these exercises together.

Our doctor told me that Eddie spent too much time in his playpen and did not get enough cross/crawl patterning. Children need the development phase of crawling to develop the brain's neurocircuitry to cross the midline. When he was in elementary school, Eddie and I played games of chase, rapidly crawling around the living room. We imagined we were animals in the woods. We marched, swinging alternate arms forward. My dyslexia improved, as well as Eddie's.

I applied the concepts of DeBono's 'Lateral Thinking' in my Creative Learning Programs. It uses both the left and right brain hemispheres. The emphasis is not on just getting the right answer. The first step is to gather the related facts to obtain a creative solution. Flexibility in thinking is important in developing new ideas. Lateral thinking defines the focus and lets the related facts incubate so new insights flash into the mind.

Imagery is a creative flow incorporating change. As a child, I used to imagine what my brain looked like inside and imagined it was organized so it would work right. I had both of my sons, my daughter, and my students visual optimal wiring of their brains as part of the psycho-cybernetics imagery. At that time, I didn't have the advantage of Dr. Lawlis's 2006 research, but I felt visualization worked to change brain function.

His scientific research later proved another phenomenon the brain is capable of in his book, *The IQ Answer* (2006). A person can get stuck in a repetitive brain wave of unproductive behavior. This psychological process of rewiring the brain at the cellular level is known as 'Neuroplasticity'.

Dr. Daniel Amen pioneered this field over the last twenty years. His book *Change Your Brain Change Your Life* (1996) shows how to take care of your brain in better ways. He developed a breakthrough program to conquer anxiety and manage impulsive behavior. These books later helped me in my personal life and my students.

Patt Lind Kyle, MA, is another author whose innovative writing I discovered later in life to balance my brain waves, emotions, and thought patterns. She is a former professor and founder of a learning assessment company who wrote the book *Heal Your Mind, Rewire Your Brain* in 2010. This breakthrough teaching not only gives scientific discussion of the anatomy of the brain but also offers detailed techniques to access the centers of the brain for optimal function. Her brain wave CDs have a binaural beat and mental tools to promote brain synchrony to reduce harmful thoughts, anxiety, and stress; the videos on her website incorporate the benefits of color therapy and journey to other states of awareness. www.PattLindKyle.com/meditations

Having order in daily activities is important to organize and balance brain function. Learning responsibility is a part of the neurological development of brain cognition and maturity. I gave my children accountability to develop problem-solving and rationale skills. There was a certain time for each chore to be completed to get the reward. This shaping technique was an excellent motivator.

I did some trial and error setting up the optimal training program. Eddie had missed several rewards, and I was objective about letting him pay the consequence for his own choices and behavior. As I got more organized, so did my children. Using a reward system increased Eddie's motivation, and he began working more effectively. Lisa had a noticeable improvement, and Trevor maintained his high level of self-discipline and consistent good work habits. Brent was living with his dad in Plano, TX, during this time.

I began getting the children to bed at least one hour earlier at 9:00 p.m. on school nights. We set the alarm earlier in the morning to avoid the morning rush. We had a checklist in which each child was to lay out their clothes and books for school, do their homework, and make their lunch the night before. Baths and teeth brushing were also on the checklist. Those who got to breakfast on time and were dressed properly with their rooms straightened and bed made earned a star on the Star Chart. Ten stars could be redeemed for special rewards in addition to the money earned from their chores. This was an automatic process based on Our Family Rule Plan. There wasn't rebellion and anarchy. Cooperation was based on respect and teamwork in group projects and family play times. In reflection, at age eighty, this seems rather extreme, but it worked in the 1970s and 1980s. We live in a different world now, but I still feel children need structure and personal responsibility to find pride in accomplishment and self-discipline.

Behavioral Contract

During our Sunday night Family Council Meeting, we designated 'individual target behaviors' to reach our personal goals. Each family member had a personalized list of their specific behaviors and activities to reach their chosen goals. I never set up expectations for others that I didn't expect of myself. We each set up our own target behaviors. I began to look for positive steps for improvement in each family member's progress. The focus on small improvements encouraged improved behaviors.

These Were My Primary Goals

My goal was to have more relaxed, playful times with the family. I wanted to give my children a healthy start in life with happy memories and a sense of being loved and cherished. Here are my target behaviors to reach my goals:

1. Participate in outdoor activities such as walking and appreciating nature
2. Eat only healthy meals which are on my organic allergy diet
3. Create time to play and be with my children
4. Picnic at the park with family
6. Read to the children regularly
7. Set theater time for the whole family to do improvised plays and puppet shows
8. Do relaxation practice and meditation for thirty minutes daily
9. Practice my routines of sound therapy, toning, and yoga for thirty minutes daily
10. Continue my study and research for one hour daily

In my Behavior Contract, I agreed to do what was necessary to accomplish these behavior goals and have enjoyable time expenditures with the family. I signed this personal agreement I made with myself.

Results of Family Target Behavioral Project

Each family member made their own goals and behavioral contract and set up their rewards. As an overall effect of this program, I felt a considerable reduction in stress in myself and within the entire family. Communication improved. We each felt more in control of our time, emotions, and environment. The largest areas of growth were:

1. The improvement in self-responsibility in work projects
2. General level of consideration among family
3. Prioritization of activities and organization of time
4. More quality time together

I used a consistent program to reach my goals and reconstructed my behavior into a calm approach to daily tasks. This brought more enjoyment in the moment. I realized the most important factor in feeling content with my life is to have enough time to do things that are meaningful with loved ones.

I gave my children good nutrition with unprocessed foods to improve their brain function. We ate more fresh organic vegetables and only fruit for sweets. I encouraged them to be in the sun and outdoors, connecting with the energy and peace in nature. Sunshine is the best source of Vitamin D, which helps the memory center in the brain.

My research indicated that other helpful supplements to support brain function are folic acid and other B vitamins in green leafy vegetables. These nutrients increase vital supplies of oxygen to the brain and organs. I developed a program entitled "The Parent's Role". In my consultation with parents, I recommended a healthier diet, free of junk food with organic multivitamins.

In 1973, I was privileged to teach this nutrition curriculum and learning techniques in a three-credit class for teachers at Webster University in St. Louis, MO. (At that time, it was still Webster College). In the early 1970s, I taught continuing education classes at Forest Park Community College and Eden Seminary. I also taught programs at several Jewish, Catholic, and private schools in the St. Louis area and used the programs that I had developed for my family to help other families.

My Internal Battles During the Years I was Raising My Children

It is amazing what tricks the mind will play on a person to deny reality when their mind is made up about something. Despite all the challenges that I overcame and the progress accomplished with my children, my unconscious mind summarized my accomplishments as failures. I had students to tutor and was asked to teach special classes to teachers, but I faced a lot of ridicule. I didn't have any educational credentials at that time and taught unorthodox methods of addressing learning disabilities.

In 1973 my innermost belief about myself was related during a regression hypnotherapy session in which I said the following, "I feel like the littlest angel sitting at the gates of heaven with my box of offerings. Nobody wants my help or me. I am useless and inept. How could I be so presumptuous as to believe they would want me or my gifts?" I felt great sorrow.

Still in hypnotic regression, I heard my Guardian Angel say,

"You believed the false concept of yourself as incompetent and unworthy. If a person walks along radiating rejection, they are not going to feel the love of others. Your Spiritual Guides are surrounding you in love and respect. You pushed it out because of false beliefs in your lack of credibility and being deserving."

My insecurity came from the false belief that no one validated me. As I reflected on this later in life, Mother's opinion that I was inept fed into this. I could see how inaccurate this was. My self-image was not in alignment with my capability or my experience. I had unconsciously focused on my childhood teaching regarding my lack of power to do anything on my own. This had been a block to my success. I couldn't accept my worth due to the guilt of failed marriages. I blamed myself for everything that didn't work out the way I had planned. I negated my success on unconscious levels.

I felt guilty for being alive due to Mother's health issues related to her pregnancy. I let guilt drain my life force. I had the feeling there was no way I could please anyone or do anything right. It's like I took the way I related to my mother and men and expanded it to the whole world. I had to release this fallacy and see the truth of my experiences.

I lost precious time with my children trying to live up to other people's standards. I had to learn to release judgment and to live by my standards. At almost thirty years old, I was still looking for acceptance and respect, which I didn't have within myself. My life was spent trying to earn the understanding and validity of others. I tried to get respect for my performance. It was as if my inner child was saying, "See how neat I am; I am okay; see my worth?"

What I am going to share with you leaves me vulnerable, but perhaps you'll see the absurdity of these attempts for acceptance. I hope you don't waste your life on this process. I felt I had to fix other people's problems to make myself acceptable. I had a false responsibility and believed it was my job to save others from their erroneous attitudes and actions. At times, I was trying to help people who didn't even want it.

My religious training in church supported this concept of saving others. When I was eight years old, I had promised Jesus at the church altar that I would help save the world. I dedicated myself to the mission to go and save someone somewhere. Now I see I wasn't entirely doing it to help them. I was telling other people things I saw about them to help them. Even though my teaching skills were effective, at times I came across as too judgmental. When others didn't see my worth, I felt they were putting me down. I sought their understanding but got their anger. I wanted their respect, but got their rejection.

I realized a part of my zeal to help was coming from an insecurity syndrome. This was a manifestation of not accepting and not loving myself. I was looking for love and validation by serving others. Wrong motivation!

My Realizations

I realized I was depending on external things and others to make me happy. I had been looking in the wrong places. I went through a period of confusion regarding the value of money. I felt if I had wealth and prestige, I would be noticed. I thought it would bring me acceptance and validation. If someone can't give that without the outer trappings of wealth, their respect isn't genuine anyway. My Guardian Angel told me that money and power would be withheld from me until I wasn't influenced by how it affected others. I would not have it until I did not need it for my self-worth.

During the many years I was struggling financially, Divine removed all escape mechanisms so that I could return to the real source of love and joy. I was not given the opportunity to find fulfillment in money until I found joy in the more important things.

Since I didn't have money for trips and extravagant spending, I found how to be happy without these. Instead, I traveled to other realms in meditation. I took my kids camping in the woods and played the games of my youth with them. I played piano, and we sang songs as I did with my parents. My kids and I had one special song that had these words, "That's the way it is by golly; that's the way it is." This relates to the concept that you live with what you create, and we are each the master of our fate. If you fall down, get up and try again.

CHAPTER SIX

DISCOVERY

Thirty-five years old seemed to be some magical age at which I should have arrived – to what I'm not sure. I had planned that at least maturity and affluence should be mine by that time in life. Instead of this, life had dealt four divorces, leaving me the sole breadwinner for my four children. My main goal was to attain peace of mind and self-acknowledgment.

My life had been a turnstile of events and changes up to that point. I had experienced much defeat and a good measure of success. Being the kind of person who actively plunges in, I had managed to cram a lot of life in these years. I wanted to reach the age of thirty-three in hopes my parents would realize I was an adult. That wasn't on the horizon at any age. It never happened. When I was fifty years old, Mother still didn't see me as an adult or validate me. I was still just Daddy's little girl.

The weekend of my thirty-third birthday changed my life and brought an unexpected level of contentment. My mother and dad came to St. Louis and took the children home with them for two weeks. My dream was to 'put care to the wind' and take an excursion alone. I didn't know my destination that evening when I left our empty home. My only plan was to meander through the Ozark Mountains of Missouri, stopping at whatever looked interesting.

The weekend started with a bang at a July 4th fireworks display. I have never seen one to compare. As I lay on my quilt in the city park with a multitude of other people, the whole sky exploded with glorious colors. The orchestra was playing the soundtrack from 2001 Space Odyssey. It seemed I transcended into the splendor of light and sound.

The next evening brought a movie that set the tone for the rest of my life. I saw the musical *The Lost Horizon: Shangri-La*. It is about a civilization that has evolved to a state of harmony and peace. The one creed that they lived by was to be kind and gentle. There was no jealousy, guilt, hate, or violence. There was no need for police and government intervention since the law of the land was unconditional love. The ramifications of a culture living under the 'law of love' impressed me. Peace can result. I thought about the meaning of love and how to experience unconditional love for myself.

If all the cultures over the world raised our children this way, negative feelings and actions would be non-existent. Diversity and equality would not be issues. Think what miracles we could achieve if we based the cornerstone of international peace on kindness. I believe in the philosophy of *Namaste,* which means "I honor the place in you in which the entire universe dwells. I honor the place in you which is of love, of truth, of light, and of peace. When you are in that place in you, and I am in that place in me, we are One."

Back to my excursion – I rolled the windows down and let the wind blow my hair recklessly. The sense of exhilaration and joy that such a simple thing can give is funny. I had resolved at the onset of this vacation not to hurry or rush to any certain place. Many times in the past, I have been so busy rushing toward a destination that I missed the trip along the way. At times, even the attainment of a goal seemed hollow.

It has seemed strange to me that we can all go down the same highway of life and experience it so differently. Since the time was mine, I stopped at a state park and looked at a fresh-water spring. I reflected, vowing to live more naturally. I decided to move the kids to a farm when I got back home. I didn't want them to miss the experience of being in day-to-day contact with trees, hills, rocks, and wildflowers.

Midway through picking a bouquet of wildflowers, I questioned my motives. Was it to tell someone I picked wildflowers to impress them or because I enjoyed the beauty of the flowers? As I laid the flowers on the front seat, I wondered why something wild dies when taken out of its natural habitat. There had been times when I felt like I was in a cage. I had to go my own way at those times and follow my heart. I had to feel the freedom of the quest for more excitement and joy in each moment.

I remembered my life as a little girl when others said, "Oh, isn't she cute?" I realized I was still living my life for the enjoyment and approval of others. Life should not be a performance but an experience to be savored. I gave myself permission to live the rest of my life for my values instead of living for other people's ideas of success. Maybe these people are the 'Joneses' we are to keep up with. I still don't know who 'they' are.

Back on the road – I stopped at a shopping center for writing materials. If I purchased only what was on my list, I would be independently wealthy. But oh, that rose pendant necklace was irresistible! And how could I have gotten by without those sterling hair clips? There was something else – oh yes, a pen, pencil, and paper. I wish I had all the money I saved on sale prices, which enticed me to buy things that I wouldn't have paid the regular price to acquire. You know, the things that weren't on my list.

The next stop was a place called Elephant Rocks. With pen in hand, I went to sleep on my quilt near some immense rocks. Waking up refreshed, I took a trail hike through the park. I discovered a beautiful inlet of a lake not ten feet off the beaten path. Some people were walking by. As I returned to the trail, I told them about the amazing view across the water, just a few feet away, but they walked hurriedly on by.

I could never understand why people are too rushed to experience beauty, even on an outing in nature. I decided not to let it bother me anymore. I didn't want to stand in judgment of their choices and mess up mine. A man was carrying his little daughter on his shoulders. As she began to fret, he said, "Life is rough. I don't deny that." What was he teaching his innocent child?

I thought of the formative power of our thoughts and words. We bring about the reality we believe in. Our words have consequences. I had heard that concept for many years. I finally realized the reality of this on emotional levels that weekend. We mustn't think of ourselves as victims of whatever the wind chances to blow our way. All our thoughts, words, and feelings comprise us and form the quality of our relations.

Until a person exercises the right to choose a positive expression in life, he or she will be leaving the door open to negative input. We can each choose supportive alternatives. Through positive thinking and affirmations, the things we concentrate on are drawn into our lives. In this way, we are the co-creators of our reality. Our words and thoughts are formative.

My mind was snapped out of its wanderings by the winding, tedious road. The highway bustled with vacation traffic, and the lack of margin for error on the narrow roadway made me nervous. I became anxious to get to a four-lane highway for simpler driving conditions. Then I could calm down. Instead, I decided I could remain calm no matter what was happening around me.

Time out! I pulled over and stopped in a park marked Rest Area. Was this the only place I allowed myself to rest? Rushing and constant activity were violations of the code of rules that I had set for my journey. Hurrying up and relaxing was a rather silly rationale. I reminded myself that if I waited until I reached my destination to relax, I might never do it. Besides, this vacation trip had no established destination.

I had practiced meditation and progressive relaxation for many years from the teaching of Herbert Benson (1975) in his book *Relaxation Response.* I found a self-hypnotic visualization that works for me: I imagine how my body feels when I am relaxed. I tell myself I am relaxed. I sense calm water nearby. As I create the result of being calm, my thoughts no longer race ahead as they did when I was tense. I create a reality that my mind believes, and it becomes my new actuality.

Driving once again, the curves in the road seemed comparable to the troubles in life. An awareness hit me! I realized that I falsely interpreted difficulty as interesting and easy-going times as boring. I heard myself say out loud, "Some curves add spice to life." I decided curves in the road and life struggles no longer needed to be my spice of life.

In my childhood, I had my mother's role model of living in a state of crisis, external control, and drama. Instead, I decided to set up a peaceful lifestyle that held mystical adventures. I could replace difficulty with exciting, positive adventures. I didn't want to pass a crisis orientation on to my children.

The next event was a Bluegrass Country Music Festival and then a place called Johnson Shut-Ins. Here, people crawled all over rocks and waterfalls in a two-mile section of the river. I joined about one hundred others struggling from one slippery rock to another. Seeing no purpose to making life so difficult, I soon climbed to a nearby cliff top and watched the process of people pushing themselves past their limits of comfort.

It was interesting watching people work up the nerve to dive into the waters below. I never aspired to do this, so I climbed down the rocky cliff with my air mattress. Later, I questioned myself on the validity of carrying it on this adventure, for I had never made it to the water.

Finding a secluded campsite, with ten thousand other people who came out to get away from it all, can be challenging. Somehow, I was successful. Not too far away was a man and woman with guitars, and I listened to their sweet music that evening. As it got near nightfall, I looked for more wood for the fire. Wandering in the backwoods, I found an abandoned house on the hill away from the campground. After the firelight music, I went back and spent the night alone under the full Moon. Looking up at the stars lying on the ground near the abandoned house, I realized the universe seemed so overwhelmingly vast. I drifted off in my sleeping bag, thinking of the glory of nature.

Waking up to the sunrise, I could see a daisy field stretching into the meadow beside the old house. It seemed the endless stretch of fresh daisies in the early morning dew was the expression of spring and new beginnings. I still grow daisies to represent joyous living, hope, and new beginnings. I still wonder if this couple were Angels who came to teach me a lesson, and I cherish this memorable experience.

I wrote this poem about my excursion:

A Daisy Field

A daisy field is a beautiful place
to wake up on a Sunday morn.
The flower's splendor near my face
makes me truly glad to be born.
Now don't you see?
The birds, the flowers, the trees
are all meant for you and me
To find nature's beauty in the breeze

I decided to go horseback riding that morning and trotted slowly along a path with ten other people behind our guide. I was enjoying the scenery when I saw a buttercup beside the trail. As I pondered the simplicity of its existence, these words came to me:

The Buttercup

Oh, the life of a buttercup
It has the gentle rain from which to sup
No human tears or pain its care
To be and grow are it's only dare
No strain in toil or play
For its life is just for today
God blends nature with a loving force
Oh, to be in unison with this source

We're meant to be one with all life
Safe from the world's strife
Just as the buttercup gives beauty,
We also have a compelling duty

We have this life for living
To be spent in joy and thanksgiving.
When we find our place in all the flurry
We'll live as the buttercup and never need to hurry

Eventually, the horse trail led to another meadow. We let the horses gallop and then run. My hair blew in the wind. I remembered the carefree days of my youth visiting my friend's ranch in Texas. It seemed all the years of inadequacy, and the sense of failure were taken away in the breeze that enveloped me. I truly felt 'One' with all life and worthy of God's blessings. I opened myself to receive as I raced along on the horse. I was filled with the Divine's unconditional love beyond description.

A person cannot see a quality in someone else unless it is within them. Since I didn't have unconditional love for myself, I did not recognize it in others. Previously, I didn't have a reference frame for the perception of being worthy of being loved. When I acquired a new level of spiritual kindness and acceptance of myself, I saw it in others and began to draw it forth. I still had the challenge of overscheduling my days, and it took many years to be able to follow my Guardian's words of wisdom. Yet, the upcoming events motivated me to live what I was teaching others to do.

CHAPTER SEVEN

THE RUNAWAY

My four kids and I moved to a farm on the outskirts of St. Louis in Melville, MO. I had four horses and a wonderful big meadow. I married my fifth husband in this meadow. Even though he's eleven years younger than me, we had many philosophies and values in common at that time.

Life was my oyster for a few months until my thirteen-year-old son Brent ran away. My life played before my eyes that night. He was protesting the new stepfather who joined me in co-parenting with consistent rules. This curtailed some of Brent's wild tendency to set his own rules. Maybe Brent knew on some level this man was going to be in the picture for a long time. This marriage lasted nearly fourteen years with compatible co-parenting and mutual goals.

As the hours of Brent's absence stretched into an eternity, I re-evaluated my parenting and the mistakes I had made. Brent had defied discipline quietly – doing what he wanted. I was so busy working and managing four kids that I didn't monitor his activities with his friends enough. Two unified parents had brought an end to that. It was all supposed to happen just that way. Divine has a bigger plan in the lessons we learn from our experiences.

It was around 6:30 p.m. when we first realized Brent had been gone quite a while that afternoon. I was dialing the phone to call his best friend when my seven-year-old daughter, Lisa, came in the back door. She was crying and held a large paper sack. She sobbed, "I packed my things. I was going to run away with Brent, but he wouldn't let me. I didn't know where to go, so I came home." She cried big crocodile tears and wailed, "Brent has gone on without me!" Lisa idolized her oldest brother.

"Gone on where?" I asked, trying to keep my composure. Lisa began to cry harder. I held her in my arms to soothe her, but she was inconsolable. I stroked her hair and said everything would be fine, wondering if this would be true. My precious daughter had come so far from the time of her autistic retreat. She said she was to go with her oldest brother to Dallas to live with their father. I called, but he knew nothing of their plans.

We began the search by calling all of Brent's closest friends. None of them would tell me any information about his whereabouts. His friends had been a strong negative influence since we moved to the farm the year before. One of the boys was fifteen and involved in drugs, car theft, and shoplifting. I had done all I could to keep them apart, but Brent managed to sneak around and see who he wanted anyway. It is virtually impossible to control all your child's time and actions. They will find a way to do what they want and break the rules if they want. Brent always set his own standards.

It was getting dark, and a severe cold front had come in. The hours seemed to drag; the minutes stood still. My husband was out searching with the police. Helicopters were scanning the area, and dogs were searching in the adjoining woods. Recently, there was an incident on the river nearby. Two boys who were fishing had been killed by an assailant with an axe in the early morning hours. It is hard to put into words all the feelings I went through as the police continued their search through the night. All I felt was remorse, guilt, and panic as the time dragged on.

My mind went through scenarios of the worst. I pictured Brent trying to hitchhike to his father's home in Dallas, TX. I imagined the horror of him being sexually molested by some cruel motorist, who later threw his body into a roadside ditch. I recalled the news story of the teenage girl who had both her arms chopped off at her elbows and was left to die in a field. I forgot all my training about imagery and co-creation!

I considered all the possible tragedies that could be happening at that very moment. My adrenals were working full tilt. I was sweating, yet cold as ice. I had taken myself emotionally into a physical shock response. I wasn't doing anything I taught others to do. I was imagining exactly what I didn't want. I told myself to stop this and surround Brent in light. I had forgotten to practice my spiritual beliefs and lost faith.

Brent had been begging us to give him our permission to live with his dad. Why, oh why, hadn't we listened to his needs? Why had we ignored his feelings until he was desperate enough to run away? My mind went through the details of recent memories. I felt guilt and remorse flashing back to Brent's childhood, remembering times I hurt his feelings. It was as though the veils were lifting before my eyes, and I could see him more clearly. Every parent can recall some parenting infractions when you look honestly at yourself.

Even though I usually followed our family code of kind consistency, occasionally, I had been unfair, too strict, and then too lenient. There were times I had been too preoccupied with my problems to be aware of Brent's. I remember criticizing Brent at four years old, saying, "Why can't you do anything right?" I was passing down to the next generation what had been said over and over to me. I was destroying his sense of worth. Parents are often the hardest on their firstborn.

When Lisa had such severe problems, it motivated me to set routines and stick to them. I had to learn to be a better parent. My son made me look at reality through the eyes of crisis. The things parents carelessly yell at their children leave an imprint on the unconscious mind of a vulnerable child. If only I had not passed on the derogatory words my mother said repeatedly to me! Where does it stop? ---------- It stops now!

I remembered the teachings of *Psycho-cybernetics* by Maxwell Maltz. It changed my life by explaining the power of the mind. I was challenged to use my mind constructively in a real-life crisis situation. I didn't do so well. My childhood conditioning of guilt, fear, and insecurity battled with my adult studies on mind research.

My mother was the most accomplished worrier I ever knew. She was good at it. She thought it was her duty as a good parent and concerned person. The martyr and victim patterns she had were a role model for me to let my mind go into the worst possible scenario. I went back and forth. I caught myself thinking this situation might be worse than it is in my thoughts. Then my spiritual and physiological teaching kicked in, and I went back to surrounding Brent in a protective bubble of rainbow light.

Only time would give the answer, and the hours seemed to stand still! I looked at my watch. It was 5:00 A.M. Unable to go to sleep, I made some hot tea. Lisa got up, and so did Trevor. Even my youngest, Eddie, who was two years old, woke up at 6:00 A.M. I watched the clock every hour on the hour until 10:00 A.M. Still, no word about Brent!

Was it too late? My mind went through several other incidences that could have been earlier distress calls. I thought of the year Brent rode his bike off the balcony of our second-story Dallas apartment on New Year's Day. He was six, and his dad and I had just divorced. I spent the first day of 1970 in the emergency room all day.

The events of that New Year's Day are etched in my mind. A man was wheeled into the ER with his hand in a paper bag because it had been cut off. I never found out how it happened because I passed out. I wasn't at Brent's bedside. I woke up with Brent standing by my bed with his forehead full of stitches. He was taking care of me. I was so glad he was okay; I wasn't even mad at his acrobatics. That was then, but now what? He was there for me when he was six years old. Could I be there for him now?

Back to Brent's disappearance from our farm when he was thirteen, the police came several times and inquired if we had heard from him that morning. At noon the next day, an officer came to the door and informed me they were abandoning the search. He said, "If your son is still in the area and wanted to be found, he would have been." They believed he was hiding somewhere nearby. They had found no evidence of violence, but how could they be sure, I wondered?

I felt panic rise in my chest as I asked, "What will we do now?" "We wait," replied the officer. How could we just sit and wait? I was never good at that! My husband and I went to the house of Brent's friend. I felt he knew something but was protecting Brent's plan! Finally, after the longest day of my life, at 6:30 P.M., Brent came home. Twenty-four hours after we first began searching for my son, he walked in the back door with a grocery sack as Lisa had the day before. He looked tired and cold!

I rushed to embrace him, but he pulled away and wouldn't allow me to touch him. Brent said he planned to hide until the search was over.

Then, he would use some money he had saved to buy a bus ticket to his dad's home in Texas.

He continued with the words that I felt I deserved," I told you I had to get out of here. You wouldn't listen!" He continued, "I was waiting until dark to go so I wouldn't be seen. There were cops everywhere all day!"

"I stayed in an abandoned car in the back of the meadow to avoid the searchers," Brent continued. "It gave me time to think. Anyway, I decided to talk to you one more time about going to live with Dad."

Deliberating this decision caused another evaluation of my time and priorities. I looked at my daily schedule on the refrigerator. Although all my kids learned a good work ethic, I decided it was too strict. Having too much structure was part of the reason Brent wanted to go to his dad's.

Night-time Routine During the School Week

Homework, games, bath, evening devotional, and bedtime at 9:00 P.M. This was too constricting on everyone. No television. It was so perfect. It was perfectly awful.

I agreed to allow Brent to live with his father. Two days later, on his thirteenth birthday, he took a plane to Plano, Texas. Letting him go was the hardest thing I had ever done. I set him free to go to the place he could be happiest. I felt he'd have the best chance to grow up productively with his dad. His needs were my first concern.

This experience helped me become a more attentive mother. I was kinder, with greater patience. We spent many happy times laughing together. My kids and I are 'forever friends.' I began to appreciate the time I had with them more than ever. I savored the little things day to day. I realized these precious moments run out all too quickly.

I looked for special ways to show my love and put notes in their lunch boxes. These had a positive message for the day and always reminded them they were loved. They told me years later that their friends would ask what the note said each day. I have lots of stories of our times together on Friday Family Night and outdoor adventure quests.

We performed puppet plays and did crafts. I'll save these tales for the children's books I wrote. Now I'll take this story to its conclusion.

Three years later, Brent was an 'A' student and quite active in Boy Scouts. He had a paper route. I talked to him on the phone, and he wrote every few weeks, but I always missed his presence. We enjoyed his occasional visits.

Soon after he was sixteen, he moved back in with us in Elyria, Ohio, a small town thirty miles west of Cleveland. He randomly attended school for a couple of months. He still set his own priorities, and school wasn't one of them. No matter what restriction I gave him as a penalty, I never knew when the phone rang, if it was the school calling to say, "Brent isn't here today," or the police calling to say, "We picked up your son without a headlight at 2:00 A.M." Once, the game warden brought him in by the cuff of his neck and said, "He can't fish in the trout park without paying."

Brent had his own code of ethics. He had a genius IQ when he quit high school. He was bored and decided to get a GED. He was only sixteen, and we found he couldn't take the test until he was eighteen. He had passed the preliminary test and didn't need any tutoring classes. He got a place of his own and a job at his stepfather's factory. The night after his eighteenth birthday, he came over and said, "I scheduled the GED test for tomorrow morning. I'd like to stay here so I won't oversleep and will go in fresh with a good night's rest." Of course, I said, "Yes." He passed with a score of 96 without studying. He said he fell asleep in the timed reading essay.

Life moves on, and fifteen years from the time he ran away, Brent had a business of his own and three small children. I respect the adult he has become.

CHAPTER EIGHT
MY PATH TO INNER PEACE

I had a series of crises with divorce, moves, money problems, remarriage, job changes, rejection, and fears. The emotional and learning problems of my children were my hardest and most rewarding trials. Getting ahead sometimes involves taking a step back. As the years rolled by, my Guardian Angel showed me that my need to be validated drove me to constant activity. I had to justify my existence. I wanted to be respected as competent by others. Wrong motivation! The patterns of self-driven behaviors started when I was a young child and lasted until I was in my 70s.

I had always been a nervous person. Mother said I used to talk to my dolls as a small child. I'd tell them to hurry up because we had to rush somewhere. I used such phrases as "I'll just dash by there. I'll just be a minute. This will only take a second. I will just run in here." Mother was a typical type A behavior personality, which was deeply embedded in my early conditioning. These were phrases I heard regularly from her.

At times, I still followed Mother's patterns of constant activity and rushing. I lost things as a manifestation of feeling lost, clumsy, and scattered. I felt controlled and dominated by time. There weren't enough hours in the day. I got better at times, relaxing into the flow of unfolding events, but then I'd relapse.

My children had reacted to my anxiety, which raised the stress level of the group. They learned not only my attitudes, gestures, emotions, and other personality traits but also my fear and worry patterns. Sometimes, I was expecting the family to do as I said, not as I did. They reacted to my wound-up emotions, and I experienced guilt again.

I had to dig myself out of this dilemma to fulfill my life's mission. This has always been to have peace of mind, quality relationships, and better health. My mission also involves helping others find what's important to them. I had to set up goals to sort through my misguided use of time to accomplish this. Here are my priorities:

- To feel peaceful, calm, and contented as I go through my daily activities
- To find time to do the things I enjoy with loved ones, reading, listening to music, and walking outdoors
- To have relaxed relationships with my family members and friends
- To express my fun-loving personality with glowing health
- To be vivacious and have plenty of energy for the things I want to do
- To be an individual who demonstrates real strength of spirit and one who helps others find peace, health, and answers to their problems

When Brent moved to his dad's, I realized that I had many changes to make before this was possible. This required organizational tasks and reorienting my attitudes and priorities. I observed what I was doing, which made my world the way it was. I tracked my anxiety levels and situations that were blocking these goals. I found some specific things I could do to create change.

Each family member needed to set up personal target behaviors and goals. My target behavior was to move through the activities of the day peacefully. My overall goal for this behavioral project was to have more energy and joy in living.

Behaviors I Needed to Change to Reach My Goals in the 1970s and 1980s

I ran around on errands too much and got nervous because I didn't have the time to do the things that were important in my personal growth projects. I felt pulled between the need to get all the chores and parental errands completed, the need for proper exercise, time for my spiritual studies and meditation, and quality time for play and rest.

Life was a frantic treadmill. I tried too hard at everything. Even being happy was a project. I was always working on something productive, rushing and driving myself to complete it. I wasn't getting enough of the right kinds of exercise. Since I am extremely health conscious, this upset me. Just another thing waiting to be done!

I crowded too much into each day and got anxious, hurrying to do everything. I also got upset with myself for not staying on my healthy food diet. I had decreased energy when I didn't eat healthy organic foods. It is nerve-wracking to just explain all I was trying to do. Don't let reading this make you all wired up. I began to unwind and appreciate the beauty and simplicity of life. Join me on this journey.

Here are practices that helped me find emotional balance and reach my goals.

1. Begin the day with gratitude. List three things I am thankful to have in my life.
2. Be in nature at the beginning and close of the day, experiencing the animals, colors, sights, and sounds. The early morning mist and the night sky are celestial experiences.
3. Relax with a deep breathing pattern of inhaling, holding, and exhaling completely to the count of five several times throughout the day.
4. Walk in nature, preferably in the forest and by water daily.
5. Visualize the colors of the rainbow and gemstone properties moving through me from the rock core of Mother Earth.

My Over-all Outcome

The following principle was my guideline: There is an answer to every problem. Just try another way. Many years and many tears later, at eighty years old, I finally know my sense of worth. I no longer seek understanding outside myself. I realize that it is useless. Through self-acceptance, I have what I want others to give me. Their opinion of me doesn't matter as it did in the past.

I would say it took a while for me to get to this awareness! It literally took my whole lifetime! I hope overcoming the challenges on my path helps you find solutions to your problems. I have been my own worst critic. I hope you learn to love yourself sooner than I did. I now have balance in my daily activities and don't plan more than I can do physically and emotionally. Peace and vitality are my priorities.

My Cross Road in the 1989

Time brought another crossroad in my life: a divorce from the father of my two youngest sons. Two people can just grow apart. The love remains because you never stop loving someone you genuinely love. The daily pressures of life can come between you, and the attraction that drew you together is overridden. It seems to just get smothered by the mundane things of daily life. My journey into self was launched by this divorce.

I'll explain some highlights of this journey and the changes I experienced at that time in my life. I hope you don't have such a hard time learning your life lessons. I gave primary custody of my youngest two sons to their father in our divorce and moved to the woods near the Dali Lama's Ashram outside of Bloomington, IN. I had prayed about this devastating choice. My Guardian Angel told me it was also in the best interest of all concerned. They said it was the highest path for Patrick and Kevin and for me to reach my destiny. I had to make a choice to let my two youngest sons live with their father because he could give them more stability. I needed to make peace with all my seeming faults and failures.

Two of my older children had gone to college by the time my fifth husband and I divorced. Two of my older sons were living in California. My daughter was married. My younger sons were living in Ohio, and I was in Indiana. I had been someone's mate and someone's mother for the majority of my life. In my last marriage, I was being provided for financially. I was taking care of other people but not myself. I had no idea how to take care of myself. I had lost my role models and had to reprogram my reason for being and establish myself independently.

Going Forward with My Own Life of Independence.

My tiny cottage didn't have electricity, running water, or an indoor bathroom. I shared the community outhouse across the street and had a wood-burning stove. It looked like Snow White's cottage in the woods. I didn't own a car and had to borrow transportation every weekend to pick up Kevin and Patrick. I donated blood sometimes for money for our weekend outings. I wrote this poem right after settling into the cottage with my drum and a few belongings.

The Beginning of Being Just Me

Divorced from him
But not from them
They live with him there
Now, I'm without roles, or their care
Yet care for myself I must do
Wow! This is really new
I'm looking for deeper life meaning
Generating needed cash streaming
So innocent, it's not even funny
I look at the day as sunny
I'm a picture of health
But I'm just a little short on monetary wealth
Five dollars; no fear
I'll only buy what I hold most dear
Time with loved ones is my priority
This value puts me in the minority
Well, here I am in a new zone
I'm facing myself alone
Getting to know me will be a trick
No longer a couple at forty-six

I had to face myself in the woods. I learned to go within and always questioned authority from my inner knowing. My personal power came through self-forgiveness and self-love. I found the path after

I released expectations and external control from others. I became the force of maternal nurturing and fraternal protection to myself. I was in the process of coming into my power by taking care of my 'inner child'. I realized I had forgotten to take care of that part of myself emotionally and let others hurt this little one. I had stopped doing things the child part of me enjoyed.

I found my childhood pleasures again. I cherished the moments and had great times with my two younger sons when I picked them up to visit each weekend and when my older sons and daughter came to visit. Simple things bring great joy. We made pinecone decorations at Christmas for the treetop of a huge pine tree. (A friend cut the top off so we would not kill the tree). We did all kinds of free activities, like visiting the reptile museum and animal petting farm in Bloomington. We also wandered around Nashville, Indiana. We hiked, camped, and explored the outdoors. Kevin recently told me that I introduced him to my love of nature, and every time he goes to the woods, he thinks of me. What a gift all my family has been for me through the years.

I began cleaning big log cabins in the area for income. I imagined the corners of these rustic log homes were filled with light. I enjoyed this job and set up my own business called Handi-helper. We also did home care and some construction cleanup.

My Guardian Angel appeared to me in meditation and said I was to found a non-profit to support women in transition from abusive relationships. Handi-helper became a part of sustaining many women. We found women's jobs, safe homes, babysitters, and friends. In 1996, we got our 501C3 Private Foundation status. During a meditation, I was given our name, Sisters of Safety (SOS), because it is a universal call for help.

In 2005, my Spiritual Guides revealed we were to change the name and the mission to Seekers of Serenity. In the early 1990s, our organization helped women get jobs who needed an income to leave abusive relationships. It has been active over the next thirty years with monthly meetings. In 2013, we opened the meetings to men. The mission statement relates to how SOS helps individuals set goals to create joy, beauty, and truth from within so that women and men can be a light for our families and our communities. I had found an outlet to help others and myself as well.

CHAPTER NINE

MY AWAKENING

The 1990s opened a time of spiritual awareness. I began to prioritize my spiritual growth and practiced quiet time more than ever. This required an unwinding process to be able to meditate effectively. I used the five-count breathing cycle by inhaling deeply to the count of five, holding to five, and then exhaling to the count of five. This relaxation tool enables me to take spirit journeys in meditation. This involves going into other time zones of past, present, and future to communicate with my guides. The following is a journal of one of these experiences to heal my inner child:

The breathing relaxation cycle took me to a place within. I had the following scene revealed to me: *I began to see a gloomy fog around me in a vision. There is a small child who is inside me crying and saying, "It's not fair; they misunderstand me. I feel frightened that I'll always say the wrong things. I open my mouth and insert my foot."*

I see myself dancing a jig throughout my life to please others. They walk away, look back, and laugh with a smirk. I see myself running desperately from place to place. I am trying to get in touch with my Guardian Angel's love, but I feel undeserving. I have a recurring memory of my dad's words. It's too good to be true." I see the thought as separate from me."

My Guardian Angel told me it was not my thought and to let it go. I feel tense. I asked how to get free of this belief. I felt myself being drawn into the mental cave I had retreated to throughout my life. I feel safe here. I withdraw to this place when I don't like situations of conflict in the external world. An Angel came to me and said her name was Serenity. She will be the special Guardian for my inner child. Serenity said, "*The reality others have of you is an illusion like paper-thin tissue floating in the breeze.*

Serenity told me that my inner child is named Amber Grace. This little child inside me had always let others take me places that I did not want to go. It took me into the depths of what I would call hell. I was shown the dark side and told I was given the rite of passage to the Light. I am to remember that we each carry the Divine Light. Serenity reminded me, "Never abandon Amber Grace again." I promised her and my adult self I would take care of us. Then, I returned to my alert state in my cottage.

A Return to My Youth

I knew that when I met the next man in my life, he would help me find something I had lost. He was twenty-three years younger than me. Yet, in our short marriage, I found a unique relationship with myself and my inner child. My young husband seemed to be the embodiment of an ageless being who will always be young. Finding his unique humor, he could have fun in the most mundane happenings. He found delight in walking in the woods or watching a twig twirl in a stream. I seemed to know him from another time.

My sixth husband and I created magical ups and downs. I never liked to take any kind of stimulus or mind-altering substance to have mystical experiences. I enjoyed time travel and altered realities during meditation. Drugs haunted my young husband at that time in his life. This destroyed any chance of our relationship's survival. He was Peter Pan, the eternal child, I wanted a grown man. He was a test to see if I still needed to prove my worth. He was a test to see if I was protecting Amber Grace. We both had to learn to let one another be free to follow our own path. I realized I had written this poem for him seventeen years before we met:

Friendship

If I offer you my friendship
What will you take of it?
Will you say, "If you care,
Then you have to do this, or be there?"

Will you feel you own me?
For this cannot be
If you hold a rose tightly, it will die
A bird without wings cannot fly
So, take as I offer you the sun
Give me wings to do what must be done
The limit we will find in the sky
Our friendship true and tried

My Spiritual Rite of Passage

The world of darkness seems to keep touching my life over and over. While I was waiting for my young husband to come home from doing drugs one night, I was taken to a place that some call hell. I feared for his death and pined for his love. We had a major fight just before he left. No amount of beseeching would stop him from leaving. I was trying to open a place of communication with him. He was trying to provoke a fight so he could go out. Every time I fell for his games to get away from me, I found myself crying and filled with feelings of emptiness and misunderstanding.

Recently, a dog just appeared on my doorstep. I felt she was the reincarnation of my beloved childhood dog. I named her Lady. I had looked for the owner, but no one had responded to the ads. We were there for each other for that space in time. I knew I couldn't leave this Earth and abandon Lady. I was all she had! I felt her closeness that night when I felt nothing else. Lady helped me make it through this transition when all I wanted to do was die. I erroneously thought suicide would stop the unbearable pain.

During these times of abandonment from my mate, I found comfort and peace when I meditated. I will relate one of these spirit journeys:

As I meditated to find inner peace, a level of deep hurt was revealed. As I went deeper within, I saw a domain of darkness through a portal. My Guardian Angel Serenity said, "I can't go there with you, but remember you are the Light." I descended into a dark, eerie place with skeletal forms and screeching sounds. Snakes began to swarm up to me as soon as my feet touched something solid. I had a flash of light in my chest as I remembered the Angel's words. I began projecting this brilliant light through my Heart Chakra. The snakes immediately recoiled backward and evaporated. The whole realm began to fade and popped like an illusionary bubble.

I was shaken but felt empowered with the awareness of the force field that was called in by the presence of the Divine Light. I finally accepted that I truly am this Light, as are all others. All we need to know is that we have this energetic vibration within. I set a goal to live in the presence of the Divine Light. It was many years and many trials before I was able to stabilize this, though.

The Tree's Message

That evening, I wanted to die from rejection. I called in my Guardian Angel Serenity, and took a walk in the woods across from our basement apartment near the college campus in Cincinnati, OH. I sat beside a tree and asked about death. This was the tree's message regarding death.

"There is no such thing as death in the way that humanity perceives it. There is a crossing of the thin veil into another dimension. The soul and the energy go on, as well as the learning process. If a person commits suicide, they are stuck in the crack between worlds until their normal lifetime would have ended on the Earth."

I truly believe my childhood dog came through time from the Rainbow Bridge when I needed a friend to keep me from ending my own life prematurely. My new dog, Lady, disappeared a few days later. She was not on her lease when I went out to get her in the yard. Someday, I know I'll see her again on the other side of the veil.

The Reassurance

I was shown in meditation later that night that my marriage was meant to end. It was unbalanced, with a focus on our worst traits and weaknesses. *In the vision, I saw an American Indian shield of red feathers. I heard the words spoken firmly and loudly by a Chieftain saying, "No More!" Then I was shown a shield of black and white with very high balanced energy which represented the marriage in my destiny.*

I woke up in a cold sweat and knew I would come into my personal power by integrating masculine and feminine traits within myself. The next morning my young husband finally came home. When I confronted him about being gone, he yelled I was acting just like his mother.

He angrily broke the Y-shaped stick in half, which represented our union. I felt energy explode as he ripped this totem apart. I saw red and orange flames of fiery anger burst out of the vortex of his hands. He went out again, and I cried one last time for him. Our life together was over. I filed for divorce right after that to save my sanity. Divorce is so painful. Why did I try again? I wrote this about my encounter with my 6th husband.

Regrets of Youth

Why didn't he want the bliss we could have had?
Running away in delusions – he left me sad
Alone he walked this Earth
Seeking other outlets for his mirth
His fear of entrapment brought the end of us
Why didn't he see what we could be without all the fuss?

I have shared my poetry and plans in hopes of stirring awareness of the lessons you can learn in your encounters. I spent the next thirteen years without a mate while in the process of reaching greater self-discovery.

The First Step in My Recovery

I attended a Trance Dance Workshop in Bloomington, Indiana, along with other healing seminars to be able to move on with my life.

I had a magical experience as I danced for hours. It drew me into a meditative state, and I had the following vision:

A Dove appeared to me. I asked the Dove, "How can I become your essence of peace?" The Dove said, "You have to let go of physical things and the need for fairness and validation. This is interfering with your ability to be one with all life. You need to be flexible to be in the flow.

I set the intention at the dance to be in the flow and to become the flow. In my spiritual studies and meditation, I have come to understand that we are one with all forms of God's presence. I asked my Guardian Angel how to maintain this state. I began the breathing focus and had a revaluation as I simply relaxed into this unity with all life:

In this meditation, I began to feel at one point that I was a Dove and was looking out through the bird's eyes. I felt the essence of the Dove as a gentle, fragile sense filled me. It seemed I was a Dove jumping from one branch to another, and I felt I was as small as this small bird and had a beak. I felt straw scratch my legs as I entered a nest woven of material scraps and twigs. While I was experiencing life as the little Dove, I nestled my head under my wing in the bottom of the nest and was sheltered from the wind and cold. I felt the warmth of wings surrounding and protecting me.

I had other experiences in mystical unity with all life. I was the essence of the Wind, a Sunrise, a Snowflake, a Tree, and a Deer in my book entitled *Dolphins Dreaming Our Planetary Healing*. I felt close to the animal world at that time of my life in 1991. The fairy realms began to open up to me again. This dimension had been silent since my visions of them in childhood. My relationship with nature helped me heal from the pain of divorce.

I sought other constructive ways to heal my grief by going to various workshops. My friend had a round healing center located near Bloomington, Indiana. We gathered to experience healthy food, a hot tub, massage, meditation, drumming, and dancing as the evening progressed. We lay in patterns of nine and eleven to symbolize the completion of a life cycle and rebirth. Later, while I was meditating in the hot tub, I saw a circle in the ethers with brilliant colors of gold, violet, and blue. I felt it represented the power of the rainbow. I prayed for direction in my life to bring balance and wisdom.

Those attending this ceremony formed into circles within circles to turn the key to open the doorway of other realms. We were told in a group meditation that the veils had been lifted, and we could enter more of these mystical places. We danced and drummed through the night on the marble cathedral floors. We asked to open, receive, and give the highest, greater good. This fostered my time of awakening spiritually.

The New Beginning

My spiritual destiny took me to other locations to meet individuals who were in my process of learning. When I moved to California and Colorado, my two youngest sons came to my home each summer. I lived upstate from Colorado Springs. We hiked on the Elephant Rocks, went canoeing, and saw wonders at the Garden of the Gods and Seven Falls. I taught them rituals and how to make hand-sewn gemstone bags and personal power wands out of tree branches. We had great adventures getting lost in the forest and climbing up waterfalls.

Years later, Kevin related to me that this helped him become who he is as a man. Patrick said, "I think ideally kids should be raised by two parents. It's just that this isn't always the best situation. It's not a good thing to stay together when it isn't good for everyone. A couple should not stay together for the kids. When you and Pop split up, it made me grow up faster. It taught me to be my own person. It also taught me to make the best of what life hands me."

I felt a release of guilt for letting their father have primary custody many years earlier.

My travels took me to many places to meet unique individuals who were my teachers. I made a cross-country trip alone in 1992. Off I went to begin an adventure which far exceeded my wildest dreams. I camped along the route to Los Angeles and planned to go up the coast to Pismo Beach, CA. I wanted to visit American Indian ceremonial grounds in New Mexico and travel to some energy vortexes.

As I turned on the radio, the words of a song filled my heart, saying, "Everything's going to be alright." I have never heard the song before or since, which gave me this promise. It was certainly what I needed to hear at the time. A chill went over my body as a confirmation. The sky unfurled in magnificent splendor following a driving rainstorm. To my left was a double rainbow. On my right, I saw the most fantastic peach, blue, and lavender sunset I have ever seen. I heard my Guardian Angel say that I'd be safely guided as always.

I took a detour south to Dallas, Texas. After a wonderful time visiting with my parents, brothers, and other family members, I forged on to Red River, New Mexico. My quest was to find peace of mind and claim my personal power of the yin-yang balance. I wanted to stand on my own. My goal was to incorporate the best qualities of both genders within myself. This included male aggression, strength, and logic tempered with female compassion, nurturing, and intuition. The experiences that followed helped bring this about.

The full Moon of the Summer Solstice brought immense life-changing energy. I set up a private ceremony on a deserted road, off the expressway, at midnight with my sacred drum. After drumming and chanting, I lit a red candle and incense to bring empowerment and to burn away the victim patterns of the past. After my 'Release Ceremony,' I found a campground on the next exit down the freeway.

The next morning, I went into a small town and meandered through the shops. I had lunch at a restaurant. Nothing unusual, but then the events of that day changed my life. Four American Indian men entered this small eating place, and their presence filled it with light. They said they had a band that played at a local club and took people on tours of the area.

I signed up for their group mountain tour the next afternoon. The guide invited me to go to happy hour with their band and then watch a pool tournament at the local Western dance hall. I checked with my Guardian Angel and got verification to go with them. Remember, this was thirty years ago in what seemed like safer times.

I pitched my tent by a mountain stream and joined his band members later. Cowboys can kick up their heels and two-step into the wee hours of the night. I began talking with the two male singers in their country band. The lead vocal had a sparkle in his eyes that emulated from the center of his childhood joy. The other singer possessed such gentle sincerity that I wanted more time with their magical energy. Perhaps it would give my little inner child strength to carry on.

The band's singer spoke of his philosophy of life. He said what I needed to hear. It is now my creed and priority of focus, "Happiness is a decision one makes. It is a commitment to the priority of remaining positive no matter what life brings each day."

Just being around Billy's lighthearted, joyful consciousness was infectious. It reminded me of the power a person's mood has on those around them. I reaffirmed to be the energy of the Divine Light and bring sunshine to others' lives. Feelings are contagious, and I want to spread kindness, peace, and joy. I made myself a promise to make my words and thoughts loving so they would bless and uplift those I touch.

A few of their American Indian friends joined us. They talked to me about Indian rights and their mission to work for the reservation's political freedom. At first, they thought I was just wearing trinkets of feathers and jewelry while putting on a surface interest in the American Indian culture for show. I assured them of my goal to restore the philosophy of 'Oneness' and respect for all life. We arranged for me to hear more about their traditions and, on the mountain tour, to hike up a nearby sacred mountain the next day.

An eerie misty fog surrounded the foot of the mountain as we began our climb. An older man they called the 'Peace Maker' was leading our trek. He was quite an interesting philosopher and told me I would someday find what I was seeking. He also said I'd need the staff I found along the way for bracing up the steep incline. The air was thin, so we had to stop and rest periodically. We were still several hours from reaching the top.

I sensed an incredible power as we sat in the silence, resting. When we started our climb again, I commented on being so overloaded in life that I literally ran from place to place at times. The Peace Maker laughed as he said, "You cannot run on this mountain, or you won't be able to breathe." He had such a lighthearted, practical approach to problems and spoke in terms of simplicity and truth.

I asked our other guide, Rooster, how he got the nickname. With a twinkle in his eye, he said, "I am quite a high stepper on the dance floor. People say I look like a rooster whirling my partner to the music." Rooster taught me the wonderful lesson of knowing one's importance. He related," If someone feels their worth, they won't need anyone else to find happiness." He seemed so self-contained and whole within. He stated, "You just have to know how you feel and what you are looking for. No one can find it for you," He asked if I knew what I was seeking. He said, "No one can find it for you."

I answered, "No, there is just a void. I don't think I'm trying to fill it with another person, but I'm at a loss to understand what it is." The old man touched my forehead, and without words, he transferred a profound gift. After several minutes, he asked, "Now, do you know what it is? I just gave you a peak at it."

I thanked him for the blessing he had shared of unconditional acceptance. I realized my need had been to be cherished by just one individual regardless of my performance. He had given me the capacity to cherish myself just as I am. Tears welled in my eyes as I felt no need to achieve anything or prove myself. I saw the uselessness of driving myself for acknowledgment, perfection, and validation. It was as if all of nature began to speak directly to me.

As we climbed higher up the mountain, I looked to the left, and a little fern caught my attention. I was drawn into its energy and felt it communicate, *"You don't have to prove anything. Know your strengths. Claim your power."* I told this message to Rooster and he said, "The branch is saying to be yourself. Do what you want to do to be happy."

At our next rest stop, we sat still as a gentle rain began to fall. Rooster told me to listen to the lesson of the rain. It spoke to me with this reminder, *"Touch with a tender caress. Stop pushing ahead and being driven to get results. Walk your path gently without expecting others to meet your expectations."*

I looked up to see an immense tangle of fallen trees and roots upturned on the mountain. I heard, *"Stop struggling and live with patience. Enjoy each moment. Just as the delicate rain droplets fade and blend as they touch Mother Earth, time is fragile."*

The strength of the wind was present in what appeared to have been an earlier battle of the Titans. I touched the bark where lighting had previously left its mark of power. It transmitted a message as it spoke to me, *"All passes into a new form. Remember the lesson of the fern about savoring life. Have confidence and know your worth."*

I saw the aspen where the deer and bear ate at the base of the trunk. Connecting with this energy, these animals related their message, *"Call the races back to their roots to preserve the ways of their ancestors. You have been born to remind others of the unity and diversity of the many cultures. Families need your message to raise the next generation wisely. You are called to teach respect for all life. Each person carries the gift of healing. Help them recognize their spiritual essence within."*

Rooster and I sat under a tree limb that had formed an arch looking somewhat like a rainbow. We did some drumming and chanting as the clouds circled the top of the mountain's crest. The arch-shaped branch seemed to communicate these words to me, *"You are the beginning and the end. You are the totality. The circuit is completed in the power of your circle."*

The Peacemaker told me to hug the large trunk of the tree and gain its wisdom for problem-solving. As I followed his directions, I experienced a level of inner peace I had never felt before. The tree explained, *"Each person is the completed whole. There is no need to seek the missing parts of one's self in others. There never was."*.

We found our way down the summit in reverence to the gifts the sacred mountain had shared silently with us. When a person learns to feel their connection to nature and use it in balance with the intellect, a synchronized self emerges. I allowed myself to feel the goodness of my *True Self*. This is who I am at the core of my being. This is the truth of myself that is not affected by other's opinions and programming of me.

Sunbeams, rainbows, and trees are such good teachers! During my journey up the mountain, I truly found peace through my connection to all life forms. My search for my self-worth was enhanced as more of my life purpose was revealed. Saying goodbye the next morning was not easy. I told Rooster, "There are some experiences during one's life that are never forgotten. I will always embrace the lessons of our time together."

I had learned to embrace my tears and to let them go into Mother Earth.

CHAPTER TEN

SPIRITUAL INSIGHTS

I had been told by my Guardian Angel that part of my mission is to help the children. First, I had more work to do for the children in my own family and for my inner child. Before my mission came into view, I had to let go of the co-dependent concept of believing happiness was dependent on someone else. We are all responsible for creating our joy, peace, and connection to our inner power.

I had to release other people and let them be responsible for their own choices and actions. I couldn't save them. I erroneously learned as a child in church that it was my responsibility to save people. Otherwise, they were going to hell, and I didn't want that on my head. I didn't want anyone to go there. I lost my focus trying to fix others. I had to learn to let go, let others make their own choices, and pay the consequences.

The hardest place to apply this principle is with your own children. There is a gentle balance between training your children's values and knowing when to let go as they make their own decisions. I later read, "Good parents give their children roots and wings. – roots to know where home is and wings to fly off and practice what has been taught them." This was written by Hodding Carter in 2014.

The only way to go deeper into self-discovery is to walk away from what you think you are so you can be who you truly are. It is necessary to let go of what you have been told you are. These concepts are your walls and your fences – your borders and boundaries. The quest up the sacred mountain in New Mexico had opened the door to my heart. Before I would be ready to launch my mission, I had some personal clearing to do. I needed to go deeper into my heart center to find my inner wisdom.

I have a deep love of the American Indian traditions and their connection to Nature. I'm also drawn to Eastern India's teaching of the Chakras and their relationship to one's physical, mental, and emotional condition. My life quest incorporates the study of psychology, physiology, philosophy, and spirituality. This supports my goal of learning about cultures and finding the good in varying belief systems. My life's path connects the mind, body, and spiritual aspect of the whole person.

Each of the following Spirit Journeys in meditation brought an awareness to recover my authentic self. You can use a drumstick and drum to record a rapid drum beat for yourself or have a friend drum a repetitive cadence that takes you into deep relaxation. In each meditation, use your breathing to enter an altered realm and focus on your breathing and body movement to return to waking consciousness. These Spirit Journeys were conducted over a period of years and took place while listening to a rapid drumming CD tape. For the last fifteen years, I have found Stephen D. Farmer's CD quite helpful. It accompanies his book *Power Animals: How to Connect with your Spirit Guide* (Farmer 2004).

To begin any meditation, I cleanse my vibrations by burning Sage and Sweetgrass and call in the Guardians of the seven directions: North, South, East, West, above, below, and within. I always call in my Guardian Angel, Ascended Masters, four Elements (Earth, Air, Water, and Fire), the Reiki Masters, and the special Nature Spirits and Animal Totems that are designated by my Higher Self for the Spirit Journey or Ritual.

Then, as you listen to the drumbeat, visualize yourself going down a hole to a tunnel into the Inner Earth. An Animal Totem greets you there. Follow this guide on a journey of healing. After 20 minutes, play four drum beats to signal it is time to go back up the same tunnel to complete your Spirit Journey.

Count from one to five as you return to an alert awake awareness. Journal your experience. I'd like to share a few of my meaningful journeys from this process:

Spiritual Journeys to Discover Teachers Within Ceremony to Release Co-dependency

I saw myself in a cave being led by another lady. It was so dark and sheltered that the light couldn't get through. I felt I was dependent on someone else to let in the light. I couldn't see my own brilliance while I was holding onto their light.

My Spirit Guide said, "Walk into the luminous Light and peacefully stand by yourself. Even if no one notices that you are standing there, remain in this Light. No longer let others govern your mood or dwell in the darkness with them in their problems. Let the past go and release all karma of your childhood and past lives, which carry judgment. It's time to stop repeating patterns of abandonment and lack of support. Validation, understanding, and nurturing now guide your path."

I pledged to myself that I would seek this highest guidance within. This brought the quality of courage and removed my attachments to suffering. I felt my strength within and released the need at a deeper level to reach out to others for my sense of worth.

The Light Dawning Spirit Journey

As a person becomes clear of old patterns, a greater realization can be realized. Lost dreams must be released to move on. In this meditation, I sat in the shadow of the tree and experienced comfort and peace. I began experiencing the true meaning of the Divine presence. Each person can use the following meditations to clear old patterns. I am sharing from my journal of spirit journeys, which were the process of my self-discovery.

As I relaxed with a breathing cycle, I saw a path opening before me with a brilliant light in the distance. I first saw a huge wheel spinning and felt this represented the wheel of time turning. It became a disk and then a spinning vehicle, which landed on Earth, forming a crater.

I was sucked into the hole it formed and went deep into the inner Earth's core. In the center of this core, there is a crack in time, like a time warp. I went deeper down into this tunnel of time where a blue and bright pink mystical bird appeared. He accompanied me on a journey to the 'crack between the worlds.' We went into a plateau, which holds the energy of lost dreams. This is where all hopes are trapped. The energy of unrealized 'thought creations' is stuck here. This alternate reality of loss has to be cleared before one's new dreams can manifest.

In this realm of lost dreams, I encountered the soul remnant that had split off from my inner child. I saw myself as a small child rejected and lonely in the corner of my fourth-grade math class. I went to this child, and I consoled her. I promised not to abandon her again and assured her I would not let others tease her for being different.

My inner child cried and said she did not know how to stand up and express her needs. She felt pushed off in the corner and did not know how to communicate appropriately. I had to heal this part of myself to move into my mission as my Higher Self, which is the expression of my True Self connected with the Divine..

I showed Amber Grace my heart-shaped Rose Quartz Gemstone and told her she would never be without the energy of this loving care. I promised her that the Divinity in me would never abandon her. I gave her a beautiful tiny bouquet of Daisy flowers. To represent new beginnings. With a smile on her little rosebud lips, she flew like a Fairy into the center of the Rose Quartz Heart. I was then told to claim my Divinity as a united whole being. She smiled, and I felt loving energy move into my solar plexus.

Then I saw a house in the woods. It was my dream of a health retreat center. I saw this encapsulated in a bubble that floated away. It went into the distance and burst into an explosion of rainbow colors and golden-silver sparkles. I saw the pink and blue mystical Bird create a trail of Starlight that was erasing fragments of false programming of insecurity. I released my intellectual planning and effort regarding the retreat center and allowed the flow of Supreme Source to fill my cup with overflowing bliss and joy.

My new Animal Totem brought me back to the Portal which led to the Crack Between the Worlds. This took me up the tunnel and out to the surface of the Earth. The mystical Bird led me forward into the *New Light Dawning*.

My Soul Recovery Spirit Journey

In this recovery ritual, I was reunited with parts of myself that fragmented during childhood from age six to my late teens. I recovered aspects of myself from life traumas in this sacred soul recovery ritual. I reviewed events that took place at certain ages. These were junctures and life-turning points that still held traumas. My Guardian Angel said I needed to clear this unbalanced energy to receive a connection with the totality of myself. I encourage you to set up a similar journey of your own to clear any disruptive energy.

My inner child, Amber Grace, came out of the cave she had been hiding in and formed a deeper connection with my adult self. This brought me the ability to ground myself and stand on my strength. I felt an awakening of the joy that I had been seeking outside myself.

This helped me access the deepest knowledge of traits and strength of my *True Self*. I have greater self-understanding to trust myself and my future. I had a series of visions recorded in my journal, which brought me better discernment. In the following spirit journeys, I had a life review during which new gifts of clarity were revealed:

Evicting the Energy of Anger to Express My True Self Spirit Journey during Meditation

In this spirit journey, I was taken to a path that goes back into the woods to see my friend the tree. I entered the forest and felt the energy coming up the soles of my feet. I sat under the tree and played a rapid beat on my drum.

I had a vision I was in an enchanted forest going back into a tree cove. The intense fresh smells and dampness reminded me it had just rained. As my consciousness went deeper into the vision, I reached the tree cove by the brook. I gave my special tree friend homage and heard wisdom regarding my life path.

The tree said, "*It has been many lives since you initiated a hurtful action. You no longer initiate conflict, but you are holding onto past pain. Anger has been buried deep within and is surfacing. Call it forth and dismiss it to the Light. An invading energy force is lowering the frequency of your mind, body, and spirit. It is attached to the anger in your shadow side of undesirable traits.*

I saw the dense, mucky energy filled with anger leave when I declared aloud, "I have first jurisdiction of my physical body, and this angry energy is not welcome!" I began to feel there wasn't enough air to breathe. There is a force field pressing on my chest, cutting off the airflow in my throat. That is why I felt out of control. I let another's negativity infiltrate me. I asked the tree how to get rid of it. I didn't want this in me. I don't want to be open to any destructive energy fields of anger.

The tree said, "*Take a deep breath and blow it out your pursed lips. Visualize that the dark shadow side that is being pulled out of you is turning into a silver-golden and white light. Puff out dark air on the exhale and pull your stomach in deeply on the inhale to absorb the higher White Light energy. Fill your lungs and your whole body and chakras with luminous white Starlight. Push the dark, invading energy field out the top of your head. Repeat this puffing expulsion breath three times.*

I felt energy come up through my throat. It momentarily choked off my breathing. The dark, angry energy had to go! I saw a dense energy moving upward through my limbs, my trunk, throat, and head. Angry energy and resentment were attached to my light and had not left the astral field that surrounded me.

I began to have another familiar feeling surface. I felt like I was late for something. I saw a vision of Mother rushing me frantically when I was a child. This reoccurring pattern of behavior had formed a lingering, energetic memory that continued to imprint my consciousness. It brought forth a feeling of having my life force choked out of me.

I demanded, "This pattern is to leave me now!" The disturbing, energetic experience relented and moved out the top of my head. This cleared my energy of the nervous rushing activity of my youth.

As this lower force field left, the Tree said to fill my energy with pink light and pale aqua blue light with purple around it. This formed a shield of unconditional love that glowed in my Heart Chakra and extended about three feet out from my body past my Aura. The Tree told me this protective bubble would keep any invading force fields out.

The tree explained, "You need more sleep. Get to bed earlier. Move at a slower pace and slow down your body's energy. It has been too wound up. Stop the rapid mental chatter and remain still to hear the Divine's messages."

I used my five-count breathing cycle to slow down my entire energy field. As I did this, my meditation deepened. The bright pink and blue magical Bird flew by and wanted me to go with it. It headed off into a dark part of the forest and went down into a ravine and a cave. The energy there felt like an evil presence.

The Tree said, "This destructive force cannot hurt you because you are always surrounded by the pink and blue swirling light. Maintain the energy field of this shield of balanced masculine/feminine energy. If dark forces approach you, they will instantly change into bubbles that pop. Stabilize in joy, rather than being lost in those who are outside yourself."

The Tree told me to touch it and become aligned with the purity of all life as I touched the Tree with my palms. I began to feel an inflow of golden-white light, which raised my energy frequency. This energy especially collected around my throat. The Tree said to make certain that what I say is pure, kind, and supportive to all people. I aligned with my purpose. My head began to ache slightly as my Third Eye Chakra opened. I was welcomed into higher realms and healing adventures.

As I walked on the path back through the forest to the clearing, I knew a new day of freedom of expression had been revealed within me.

Spirit Journey in Meditation to Experience My Higher Self

During this Spirit Journey, I began to feel the energy of a Celestial Being in my Heart Chakra. It established itself as the best part of me. I began experiencing a vibrating energy filling me as I became aware of being my *True Self*. I centered my thoughts on constructive energy as fear and guilt went away. I felt enveloped in peace and assurance.

The Celestial Being said, "This is your Higher Self. Allow things to work out, and know they will happen when it is time. Cause and effect is as simple as visualizing one's core beliefs. You believed in the false principle of lack, so that is what happened to you. You have let unconscious programming from your childhood cause you to believe in the possibility of loss. You also believed in the illusion created by the collective consciousness of erroneous thinking. This cut off the unlimited supply of bounty and inheritance, which has always been yours as a being of God's grace. Each person is a treasure in the eyes of the Divine. Let go and enjoy the protection and nurturing of the Supreme Source."

On that day, I acknowledged the Divine as my substance and my support. I acknowledged the presence of divinity within me as my *True Self* communed with this essence of unconditional love in my Higher Self.

Vision of Prosperity and Co-creation
Spirit Journey in Meditation

I began to open myself to stand in luminous White Star Light with my independence and the power of healing and abundance. I became conscious of an inner presence of the abundance of true wealth. I realized the balance of masculine/feminine Divinity was generating infinite prosperity within me and felt the power of co-creation, which holds the energy of unconditional love. I began to feel pinwheels of energy that represented true wealth. I was in the center of one of the pinwheels, and it expanded as I became the size of the Universe. I became One with all as a co-creator of my desires.

The guardian said, "Your inner supply is instantaneous and consistently manifests according to your thoughts and desires. Your only responsibility is to be aware of this truth. Let go to feel worthy to receive abundance in your life and affairs."

I became centered in my Higher Self as I turned over my relationships, career, and finances to this Supreme Source within. I felt a magnetic pull lifting me into an energetic force field, drawing what I need to complete my mission. There is peace in this knowing.

I then felt energy expand from within my Heart Chakra. It seemed to reach outward to draw this magnetic force in the flow. I now understand that the radiation of this creative energy is continuously pouring forth from Divine consciousness.

This source of prosperity is individualized as the *Higher Self* of each person. Divine within us is lavish, unfailing abundance connected to the rich, omnipresent substance of the Universe. In this vision, I realized that no person, place, or condition outside myself is the source of my supply. My awareness of the Divine within me is my continual supply.

Our consciousness of the truth is unlimited. This applies to every individual. We have only to align ourselves with the energy of the vibrational matter of abundance to become immersed in its flow. The following are steps of this Dream Fulfillment Process:

Begin with a Release Ritual – Sit with your palms up on your lap. Inhale the connection of your *True Self* to your *Higher Self.* Close your eyes and breathe deeply to the count of five. Let go, saying the word "Release" as you exhale to the count of five. Surrender your life mission to your highest calling in the divine's perfect plan.

1. Say the word 'Unity.' Think of yourself as united with Divinity.
2. State a goal you want to attain.
3. Visualize what you want enveloped in golden-silver and white celestial Light.
4. Make clear present tense affirmations as follows:
   "I step into my power. I am cleared of all harmful residues. I am dedicated to my life goals and mission, and I open the floodgates for blessings to flow. "
5. Believe that your goals are already being attained. Know that the best outcome is actualizing. Release the process of how this takes place for the good of all. Close with gratitude for the flow of blessings.

Spiritual Breakthroughs
My Vision on a Spirit Journey into Unity

More mystical experiences began to happen to me in my Spirit Journeys. In this meditation, I was in another life, running in the forest of Brazil.

In this vision, I began to become one with all forms of the Divine's Presence. I was the healer and the healed. I was all Elements of Earth – the Wind, the Rain, the Sun, the Moon, the Mountain, the Ocean, and the Fire. I saw a brilliant light in the distance in the dark void. It moved closer and closer until it moved through me, and I exploded into luminous white Starlight.

I became a baby who was sitting in the middle of the Milky Way. There was nothing around me, but I felt like I was everything and everyone. I became the sound of a flute coming from an indigenous man. A dancing woman was twirling and flowing to the fluid rhythms of sound. I became the dancer, the dancer, and the song. I am everything and everyone. Everyone else is this same totality. There is no line of separation dividing us, for we are all things. We are 'ONE.'

Spirit Journey for My Call to Service from Mother Mary

Early one morning during my travels, I was sitting in Red Rock Cathedral in Coconino National Forest near Sedona, Arizona. I went into deep meditation and centered in my Heart Chakra. I received a message from Mother Mary that I feel is intended for all the Light Healers and Bringers of Light.

"I have other lessons for you. Be diligent, resourceful, and loyal. These are qualities that bring success in all areas of your life. Abundance is yours. Claim it from the ethers. Now is the time. Claim you are in the right place, meeting the right people in the flow. The Divine is calling all Earth Angels. You are each on the roll call. Ready yourselves in purity. Stop associating with lower vibrations in the Earth plane.

No longer use their measurement and standards for success and worth. You are worthy in our eyes from on high. Your life has been chosen to benefit others, and fortune will be a by-product of rendering your wisdom and gifts to more individuals. Stay in the presence of the luminous white Star Light, and remember this is your true essence. Be that which you are. Your gifts will be used to encourage others who need to know their worth, values, and priorities. Call for helpful relationships in all areas of your life, including personal, friendship, business, and social settings. Do all that you do in the name of love and harmony. Blessings will be brought to you in the Divine timing."

The motivation for my cross-countries was to visit family and stop along the way to savor the beauty of nature. On one of these excursions, I meditated beside a tree near the edge of the Grand Canyon. I wanted to be filled with the fullness of this majesty. I called upon the strength and magnitude of nature and felt a new level of unity. I spent several hours there integrating my mind and the choices that were before me.

A squirrel came rather close and just sat up, looking at me eye to eye. A line of mental communication opened between us. The squirrel telepathically related, *"Our species is so busy because we are planning ahead. People need to do this also."*

I thanked him for this advice on the quality of preparedness. We shared a mutual respect, and he scampered down the cliff. I continued my morning reverie. It is a blessing to talk to the animals. They have great wisdom to share.

On my drive back to Ohio that evening, I stopped at a mesa and sat on the hood of my car, eating watermelon out of my cooler. The sunset filled the sky, reflecting vibrant pink on the sands. I couldn't see a single person or car in any direction as far as the horizon. It was as if I was the only person on this planet.

When I got back on the highway, several cars were going the opposite way. It seemed I was the only one going my way. Humanity often went in the other direction. This is how it had been most of my life. I was a non-conformist and had never fit the mold of society. I could feel alone in a crowded room. At that time, I had not found others like me who were 'friends of a feather'. Someday we'll meet and recognize one another.

CHAPTER ELEVEN

FINDING MY TRUE SELF

Self-empowerment is the ultimate challenge of the true follower. This encompasses acceptance of one's true worth past the guise of illusions of separateness. When a person realizes that we are all connected to the *One*, there are no lines of class, race, or economic distinction. In my meditations, I journeyed to a place of universal equality.

I made a Spirit Journey to the rapid drumbeat and journeyed to this place of union. I was part of a huge ritual of individuals wearing white robes in a realm in the Stars. We were being prepared for our life work on Earth as Light Healers and Bringers of Light.

These pure-of-heart individuals were focused on self and planetary healing. We each had to cleanse and release the darkness that came in and through us. I had agreed to experience this indwelling of conflicting energies as a part of my mission on Earth. We were assigned to transmute and integrate the shadow side and the Light. We were each given the task of balancing our male and female aspects.

I was challenged to face myself in my relationships and to ultimately discover this balance. I called upon this time in another realm when compassionate action prevailed.

My Move to Colorado

I had a feeling that I was to leave California, but my Spirit Guides didn't indicate where I was to go. My guides often tell me to start packing before I know all the information about where or when I'm going. That is typical of the way life changes have always taken place for me.

In the late 1990s, I was given the date of departure and Colorado as the location for meditation. But where in Colorado? It was one week before the date I felt I was to move. I had five people say, "I heard you are moving to Colorado. You must go to Crestone."

It was as if my Guardian Angel was saying to go to this location, and so I struck out for Crestone in my Toyota camper. When I got to the sign on the highway that pointed to Crestone, all I saw was a large mesa and mountains in the distance. I stopped at a gemstone crystal shop on the turn of the road and asked how far it was to Crestone.

They told me it was the small village at the foot of the mountains that was visible in the distance. There was just the open mesa between me and the mountains. The owner of the crystal shop said there were UFO sightings and strange things reported in the area. The mesa was considered sacred ground by the Indians. None of their generations had fought battles on the mesa or lived there.

I asked what work and housing there was nearby. and she said, "We only have the spa down the road and a campground." I got a job at the spa as a massage therapist and had the perfect place to park my Toyota motor home at the campground. I was thankful for the certification I received at the Pacific Coast School of Massage years earlier in CA.

I met several special people living in Crestone. They had values similar to mine. They honored the land and one another in the community. I saw what true compassion for others is like on the larger scale of community.

Things I learned in Crestone, Colorado

1. Look deeper than appearances for the true nature of a person.
2. When you meet another individual, take time to get to know them.
3. Psychic is not spiritual – environmental concern is not necessarily spiritual.
4. Listen more than you talk.
5. Find the silence within so you can hear the truth.

7. Visualize yourself doing your chosen career to manifest cash flow.

8. Many times, a lesson is not the one you think it is going to be.

9. Relax into the Divine timing.

10. Stop struggling against the flow.

11. The future holds adventure and joy.

12. Relax into the awareness that the Divine is leading and protecting each of us.

13. What you resist becomes a battle, zapping your energy.

14. Interact as a secure person.

15. Claim your right of blessings untold.

16. Affirm your place of harmony in the Universal Plan.

17. No one is superior or inferior.

I enjoyed my time in Crestone, but it passed quickly, and another phase of my life began. I have had a connection since I was a child to converse with different forms of nature. The rocks and gemstones hold ancient knowledge and wisdom of the future. I listen and encourage you to do so as well. Rune Stones are ancient alphabetic symbols first used by people of Northern Europe many centuries ago. I started doing Celtic Rune readings about fifty years ago by casting them and interpreting their messages.

An American Indian man came to me for a Rune Stone reading. Meeting him changed the way I experienced messages from the Gemstone Guardians. He asked to do a blessing for me and said I would have a vision in three days that would enhance my gifts.

A few days after the blessing, I had a vision of a huge wheel and saw a Rune stone cast into the center of the wheel and others to the north, south, east, and west of this in a circle. I was told to face north to interpret the position of the stones. I was shown in this vision that the lay of the Rune stones represents a period of time with upcoming events in your life. The stone in the center is the main issue that you are dealing with at this time. The stones in the lower half of this circle indicate the main events upcoming in the recipient's life over the next twelve months.

The Rune stones in the position of the right or east of this center stone relate to the current time. The stone in the south reveals six months from now, and the stones to the left of the center stone, or west, indicate one year from now. The stones in the northern half of the circle represent spiritual guidance. Each person can look to the future for one's self. All knowledge is within, and the important thing is to be fully aware of every present moment and release the outcome to the highest knowing of the Divine.

Set up a sacred altar with crystals and other gemstones. To do a reading for yourself, get in this quiet place and center yourself with a five-count breathing cycle. (Inhale to five, hold five, exhale to five counts, and wait for five. Counts.) Invite the Guardians of the Gemstones and your personal guides to communicate with you. Request information that would be helpful in the next year of your life. Ask for guidance to be sustained and protected in this process of your highest life unfoldment. Then, cast the Rune stones.

You can purchase Rune stone sets, which will have a guidebook for interpretation, at most gem stores. I had more adventurers in Colorado that I will tell you about later.

Time moved on, and my life path took me back to college in Yellow Springs, Ohio, to get my Master's Degree in 2005. I had a double major, one in Health and Wellness and one in Community Change and Civic Leadership. At times, I felt my left-brain studies robbed me of my right-brain creativity. I did home care for the elderly to provide for myself and studied long hours into the night. I decided to get an outlet for social contact.

My dream of finding the right mate was explored with my 7th husband, who was almost twenty years older than me. We met at the Senior Center in Dayton, OH. He was a cavalier Englishman who still knew the gallantry of an era gone by. We laughed and enjoyed plays, bowling, dancing, and eating out when my busy schedule permitted.

I told him of my goal to set up a health retreat when I graduated with my Master of Arts degree. We married in a small ceremony in his backyard with family and friends. In 2010, after my graduation, he purchased twenty-six acres of land in Kentucky for a health center. There is a time to go on with life even though someone you love has crossed to the other side or moved far away.

We moved with two 24-foot moving vans and drove under a double rainbow on Summer Solstice in a rainstorm to begin our adventure. I felt it was God's sanction. Many times, through the years, I have been given a sign that I made the right choice and am on track with my calling. This sign can be a Butterfly or Dragonfly landing on me. Sometimes it is finding a dime in unexpected places reminding me I am provided for. Sometimes it has been a message of encouragement by a Deer in the Forest or one of my Tree friends.

Everything in my life was meant to happen to bring me to this location. I found my 'True Self' and finally met my 'friends of a feather.' A few years later, not long into our plans to develop this land in Kentucky, doctors found my husband had 4th stage lung cancer. Our priority changed directions into his 'cross over' from this life into the next. I wrote him a closing message and poem of parting:

Closure with a Loved One

This is a message to those who are no longer in my life: I will continue to surround you in Rainbow Light to be strong in your path and full of blessings.

I Want You to Know I Love You

Death brings the sorrow of wasted time
Sweet as the morning dew
Leave the memories of me with you
The reaper brings peace sublime
As spirits come to claim your soul
The cleansing release makes us whole
While surrender purges this pain of mine
Breath labors life's conclusions
All is just an illusion
Death is but the horizon I'm told
Ongoing the bond we hold
As you go on your journey without tarry
One message please carry

Our love was touched by Cupid's dart
Which leaves sweet memories in my heart

Living with Myself

I am a fighter and a survivor. The truth is that survivors can heal and even thrive. I keep coming back up to the surface each time I dive into the depths of life. I am the phoenix that flies out of the ashes. To regain my life, I had to let go of the pain of times lost for love. I am grateful to those who acted as a mirror to reflect what I needed to see within myself.

I promised my inner child, Amber Grace, that I would take better care of her. I had to remember who I was in a relationship instead of losing myself. I wrote this poem, which summarizes my new path:

Vision's Melodies

All those years
All those tears
Coming first is the laughter
Then the pain, but now it is after
Call an end to the fears of rejection
Were they all just my reflection
Now where does my destiny lead
How do I answer their need
Spirit sings on the wind
Hope! This is what it will send
There are people seeking wisdom's seed
Hearts that plead
I saw a vision of myself in the morning sun
My voice spoke triumphantly through what is to be done
Music awakened my soul to the love of which the Divine spoke
In journeys, the weaver spun a magical cloak
Tones hearken that which is right

Memories of dreams held tight
A tear leaves my eye
Upon Mother Earth, it falls with a whispering sigh
To dust returns all sadness and pain
And I am freed of struggle and strain
My vision brings the gift of sight
And I am reminded…We all are light!

Going On

I took an upgraded class in my Reiki training and began teaching Holy Fire Reiki Master Certification for the next three years. I also taught others to do Spirit Journeys in meditation with sound and color vibrational healing and gave Medicine Wheel Rune readings. Eventually, I sold the property we bought for the Health Retreat Center and went on to the next chapter of my life. I dedicated myself to holding higher energy and functioning as a Light Bringer, sharing the Divine Light. It was time to develop another level of my evolution. Studying and meditation in nature were again my guiding process.

In my studies, I was introduced to a book entitled *The Heartmath Solution* by Doc Children and Martin Howard, with Donna Beech (1999), which is an excellent reference for breathing and imagery benefits. I found this extremely helpful, along with a process called *Havening* developed by Ronald Ruden, MD, PhD, and collaborated with his twin brother, Dr. Steven Ruden, a certified hypnotist and doctor of dental surgery. This is a psychosensory process that stimulates feel-good chemicals in the brain to relieve stress and traumatic associations.

I met several powerful individuals in the healthcare field, including Nurse Practitioner Kim Evans, APRN, founder of the Center for Integrative Health in Louisville. Her team of practitioners helped me resolve my long-term health issues and shared inventive techniques and nutritional options. Time passed, and I still had a lot of self-examination to do to reach my life goals.

I am perceptive and capable of determining my own needs. I like and respect myself and have nothing to prove. I am worthy of loyal friends whom I can trust to be faithful to me in all ways, and I deserve those in my life who treat me consistently with respect and consideration. One of these treasurers is Karol Flowers. (www.Amoriyah.com). We met in Dayton, but she now lives in Florida. Carol inspires others with her art and guidance. She led me to the Guardian Materials taught in Sarasota by E-LAi-sa of ARhAyas Productions LLC. This work teaches the dynamics of eternal life assertion (the way home) and has helped me understand our return to the Eternal First Field of Intelligence. (EFFI) www:arhayas.com

Donna and I met in Bloomington and have been friends for over thirty years. She became a ranger in a national park, which inspired me to be more adventurous. Donna sold her home and bought a camper. At the time, she gave me a lot of her decor. I asked if she wanted to get a storage unit to make sure she was ready for this cathartic move. She said she was sure she would never go back and was ready for a new beginning. I didn't get ready for that decision to only go forward until many years later. I lived in several places in a camper for a couple of years and now I'm settled in Georgia in a home in a wooded area. My best friend, Carolyn, and I enjoy sharing confidences and trading jewelry.

I know I can pick up the phone and call CJ or Peggy and get kind words and a shoulder to lean on whenever I need this. CJ opened her home to me on several occasions when my life fell apart. Joy and I have been support systems for at least twenty years. I stayed with her when my marriage was stressful, and I needed perspective. I stayed with her when she had surgery and needed help. They are the kind of 'friends of a feather' who are there through time for each other.

World Peace Prayer

Tree and Gemstones have always been some of my best friends. I found such comfort in their presence during the eight years that I lived on Kentucky land, which was almost all covered in a forest. I joined a group of women who taught the ways of the American Indians at the Rainbow Spiritual Education Center led by Rev. CJ Wright. Their wisdom and friendship helped carry me through several hard times.

I met a wonderful lady who was such an inspiration to me. She had been a nun for fifty-nine years and prayed daily throughout her life for world healing. I felt if she could do this, I needed to do this too. I had a Tree that I felt was the sacred location to set up a World Peace Center on the property. The Tree confirmed this. I still do this ritual daily.

I go to the wooded sanctuaries daily in person or in spirit journeys. I pray for my family and friends who have challenges. I pray for couples, companies, communities, and countries to be caring, kind and compassionate.

I ask assistance for those who are in transition in war-torn areas, those in relationships that are crumbling, those who have loved ones who are sick, injured, or have crossed over, and all who need self-love. The prayers written on signs in the Universal Truth Center bring me comfort and are part of the energy that the Light Bringers are holding in Earth's transition to a place of peace. My Guardian Angel gave me these messages, "*Prayers of gratitude are the best way to connect with the beauty of Mother Earth and the lessons nature holds.*

We are all one. Father Sky reveals the wisdom of the Universe from Grandfather Sun and Grandmother Moon and our Star relatives. We are never alone."

CHAPTER TWELVE
INTRODUCING MY FAMILY

This part of my life story is a step back in time, but it gives you more insight into who I am. My offspring have certainly brought me great self-awareness and self-love.

More on My First-Born Son Brent

I admire the man my oldest son has become. He came up the hard way, learning all his lessons by forging through conflict. He calls it 'street sense.' Each of my children reminded me of a certain animal totem and expressed their spiritual qualities. As a youth, I always related Brent to a young buck, determined, stubbornly butting his horns against any opposition. He has tapped into the knowledge of what being a man means. This is the truth past the culture's guise of a false concept of manhood. He can be tender and even cry and still knows the strength in his manhood.

Brent can keep a cheerful disposition in the face of adversity like no other. He is doing what it takes to face life's challenges and maintain a peaceful state of mind through it all. Brent has always had the most heartwarming quality that touches the core of One's being. He'd give to others beyond any measure and has a heart of gold that is kind and gentle under his rugged exterior.

He has become the man I'd hoped he'd be and still has the charm of his childhood. He's playful at the end of his day and loves to tease and bring a smile to others. Brent explained this when he wrote, "The man who can remain a boy is lucky indeed."

I wrote this about Brent in 2005 when I was assigned to write a thesis about a modern hero in my college years at Antioch McGregor University.

My Shining Son

The standard I use for determining a hero is dedication and service to the needs of others. Many have goals but never make the mark and never go the extra mile it takes to give their all. The quality of perseverance is a requirement. Motivation is the key. Optimism is the fuel that changes energy into action. I value pure intentions and honesty. My definition of true strength is to have gentle yet firm treatment of self and others.

My oldest son has all these qualities. The person I feel most qualifies as a hero is my son Brent. He has survived more challenges than most people ever have to face. Brent raised his three children against all odds after his wife died. Worry is not a word in his vocabulary. Neither financial crisis nor single parenthood got him down.

Brent has written a book of poems from this perspective entitled *One Man's Life*. He told of his pleasures, his inspirations, his regrets, his success, his children, and his gambling vices. Even though he would be considered a man's man, he wrote from his heart, showing he has the balance of a nurturer. I respect the father he became to his two little girls and his son.

I watched Brent in the hospital's special care nursery when his son was born nine weeks premature. Ernest Matthew weighed 2 lbs. 9 oz. Brent showed such a depth of love as he reached into the padded hole of the incubator. I heard my son say, "I promise to be there for you, little guy." Love shined through his eyes. Holding his tiny son's hand, a bond formed that could span any difficulties life might bring. Isn't this what makes it all worthwhile?

As he looked at Matthew, I knew there wasn't a question that he would do whatever it took to help his children make it in life. Strength was transferred to the little boy from his father's hand as he came to visit every day after work. This seemed to give Matthew the will to fight for life. With love as the motivation, all things are possible.

There was a quiet strength in Brent as he kindly administered discipline. He demonstrated his affection and let each child know they were valued as a unique person. I lived with Brent, co-parenting my grandchildren after his wife died of cancer. Those were cherished years. Tara was five, Heather was four, and Matthew was two and a half years old.

I got a close look at his parenting when I went to live with him after my divorce in 1989. Brent played with his children after an eighty-hour work week. I saw his hand on his son's head, ruffling his hair in a scuffling match. He read the children a story every night and said prayer. Every day, he woke us up singing "Zippity Do Da." He is modeling the qualities that make life worth living, which is a sense of humor and being true to himself. Brent's life depicts his philosophy: 'Live well and hard with endless passion and excitement.'

Brent never wanted to live past forty. He said he wanted to live as wild as he wanted and not pay the price with old age. I hope he will decide to keep going now that he is almost sixty. He has four grandchildren to make life even more fulfilling.

My Second Born Son, Jim Bob
(Trevor James)

The birth of my second child, James Robert, was a monumental turning point for both of us. Jim Bob wasn't due for two days, but I went into labor on the weekend. My neighbor took me to the hospital because my husband was out of town on business. The doctor could not be located. His traumatic birth became a near-death experience for both of us.

The delivery staff would not do this now in 2023, but back then, they held my legs together waiting for the doctor's arrival. As a result, my infant nearly died. I remember seeing a glimpse of my tiny son's soul leaving his body as he was finally allowed to exit my womb. I tried to follow and bring him back. I felt myself leaving my body.

The delivery room staff used a resuscitator and other life-saving procedures on us. I could see angels all around us, floating above the scene in the delivery room, with nurses and the doctor attending to our bodies below. I told my baby to stay and have a good life. I prayed for help from the Supreme Source of the Divine. An angel pulled our souls back into our bodies, and I awakened with a chubby cherub in my arms.

He had the largest head in the hospital's history in Oklahoma City. He weighed almost eight pounds and eight ounces and was only eighteen inches long. He was very active and grew quickly. He weighed thirty-three pounds at one year, and I thought he might have been Baby Huey. He looked like an adorable beachball in the suit and tie he wore in his one-year picture.

Trevor (Jim Bob) has always been a mighty go-getter. He had such upper body strength that he threw a baseball across the yard at three years old and was a Star pitcher in our Little League. He ate a healthy diet through the years, and his growth rate slowed down. He weighed in at 98 pounds in high school. Even though he was small, he played varsity golf and was on the wrestling squad. All the girls wanted to be his girlfriend and said he was a little hunk.

His self-discipline astounded the rest of our family. He would just decide to stop eating meat, or not drink, or smoke, and that was that. It was a done deal! He has accomplished everything he set his mind to do. This is one of his most inspiring qualities. He wears a smile and makes everyone feel comfortable. His career gave him opportunities to go into corporate management. Instead, he chose to follow his dream in the entertainment field. The Tiger Animal Totem qualities of vitality and willpower describe Trevor. He truly lives life like he has a Tiger by the tail and goes after his dreams with a zest. I wrote this poem about him.

Tiger

One son, now two!
I only have so much energy,
So what will I do?

Finding the joy of which to sing -
I'll make time for the love you bring.
My, how time flew!
Did I speak of the praise I have always felt for you?
You said you were proud of me that day at your school.
Did I live up to that, or let strife play me for a fool?
Trying to be perfect, you make a sensation!
So cheerful and kind. You are my inspiration.
Divorce tore my life into a shamble.
Faithfully calling, you listened to me ramble.
I am so blessed to have you.
What would I do if there had not been number two?

When your children go to school or set out on their own to forge their way in the business world, you feel a sense of urgency to teach them anything you might have missed in their upbringing. I wrote each one of my sons and daughter a letter of advice and congratulations on their life juncture into adulthood.

To My Son Trevor in College

Trevor, you are what every parent hopes their son will be. I know you will succeed at whatever you set your mind to do in life. You have been a joy since you were the quiet, happy baby, the curious toddler, and the sweet schoolboy.

It seems your diverse career has opened many doors for you to excel. Your patience will make you a wonderful husband and father. I can hardly wait to see what life has in store for you and those you love.

Trevor's Blessings

Trevor married a lovely woman with the same name as his sister, Lisa. They walked through a sparkling heart at the close of their beautiful wedding ceremony on the beach near Toluca Lake, CA. She is younger and wanted children. A few years later, they brought two wonderful additions to our family. At fifty-two, Trevor had two adorable, rowdy little boys, Dylan and Elliott. Their zest for life is exhilarating! They bought a beautiful home on the West Coast, and he is still in the television and movie business.

When they came to see us in Georgia last Thanksgiving, we cooked out by the lake and shot off fireworks. Trevor watched his wife Lisa give their little son safety instructions and smiled. He said, "Those three are what keep me going."

Trevor's Challenges

Trevor has faced serious challenges throughout his life. A few years ago, Trevor was diagnosed with basal cell skin cancer on his neck and face. This is a genetic problem from my father and me. I had surgery for a melanoma twice and a basal cell on my ear and the top of my head. I still have pretty deep scars, but at least my hair covers them.

He had a flaking of skin over his eyebrow and treated it for a year without success. He used different salves until he finally went to a dermatologist. He expected a small procedure would remedy the situation. Instead, this culminated with two four-inch scars on his neck and cheek. The larger scar on his forehead required plastic surgery. This might have caused a man with less strength to have resentment and depression. It could have caused him to be angry at a vengeful God or to feel like a victim of a hapless fate. He could have let vanity and insecurity run his life direction.

His attitude and approach to this life crisis was to turn to the strength gained rather than the harm done. Trevor took the high road and felt grateful that the physicians were able to give him a cancer-free health report. He focused on the opportunity to share the future with his wife and to raise their two young sons. He and his supportive wife faced this together. He did what needed to be done to avoid this life-threatening tragedy. I have faith that whatever life holds for him, Trevor will embrace it with passion and fervor.

After some reconstructive surgery, Trevor is the same handsome man he was in his teens. He has always been beautiful inside. An important lesson is to realize and encourage others that skin cancer isn't harmless. This is a life-threatening cancer that can spread through the body. It needs early treatment by a dermatologist in the medical field.

I have five sons and a daughter, who are my modern heroes. They have each faced challenges that could have crushed them. Instead, these situations built character. I am so proud of the life choices that they made and the strength it has given them.

My Third Child – My Only Daughter

A spiritual woman did a life reading for my daughter. She saw overlays of mutual experiences in my daughter's life and mine. She said on a soul level we have been twins, as well as mother and daughter. She said that my mother would have no part of that contract to carry and raise twins, so Lisa came into this life as my daughter. We have the same animal totem, which is the butterfly for joy, grace, perseverance, and individuality.

Most mornings, when I look in the mirror, I see myself. On a few occasions when Lisa's life was under extreme duress, I looked in the mirror and saw her face. I wrote this poem entitled "My Daughter and Me" to describe our unique connection.

Friends Forever for all to see
Yes, that is what we are to be
More than this
She's my sis
Heart of gold
Generosity untold
Beauty, grace, and dignity
We'll stand up for inequity

To My Daughter Sunshine – Our Butterfly

When I look at her, what do I see?
Myself – my twin!
No, for she is not me.

She is my friend!
Struggling to be free,
She has become a woman in her own right.
Excellence, adventure, and romance were her decree.
Sailing an uncharted course, reaching out of sight.
She wandered at times in a world of her own making.
Seeking her identity so bold.
Finding an escape from dark shadow's taking.
Someday her story will be told.
Always her sunshine has brightened the room.
She had a quantity of love that no money can buy.
She is the light of my life when troubles loom.
Lisa is my beautiful, favorite butterfly.
If I were her, I'd feel my life well done.
Class honors attained and professional skills.
Yet she drives herself on and on.
Not knowing she already processes what all seek – the love of her son,
Respect from her brothers,
Pride derived, true, and tried, from what she has done,
Devotion from her dad and mother,
Cherished time with laughter her guide.
With a heart full of love, she tries to please
Always there by my side
My daughter, so distinctly herself, each moment free
Having a gift that puts everyone at ease.
With each choice, her own way she went.
She truly lives her values without needing to please

She's a woman now! My daughter, my little girl. Where did all the years go? And yet, the clock seems to turn so slow. I've been waiting and waiting for what, I don't know. Perhaps it is for life to be as it was when our Christmas Eve celebration waited for the children to finish their naps.

Times change. Most everything is different. Yet some things remain. My little girl's grown taller, older, and wiser. She still adds light wherever she goes. I respect another part of me that is more like her.

She naturally knows things I never quite put together. My offspring is teaching me to allow things to just be. There is no pressure to make them see; whatever transpires, her love truly frees. Others never know the pain she holds, the youth she lost being a mother at seventeen. Never asking for help, she takes care of her own needs and Cory's. She finds strength within to begin again – leaving a part of her heart.

I know Lisa will succeed in weaving together a life filled with all the wonderful things she had imagined. Perhaps Courage should be her middle name instead of Christine. Lisa knows this trait well, for she has called upon courage again and again. It guides her forward on her chosen path. She is the sunshine in other's lives.

Lisa and I were both at a turning point in our lives at the end of 2014. My husband had just died, and Lisa was in the process of a divorce. She wrote this, framed it, and gave it to me for Christmas that year:

My Mother, My Friend

My mother, my friend
I want to thank you once again
For guiding me home like a beacon of hope
When I was lost in the dark at the end of my rope
Through your strength and courage, I found my own
Both of us hurting, single again yet not alone
We laughed through our sorrows and tears
While each new day dissipated our fears
We started to see rainbows, instead of the rain
Feel the sunshine instead of our pain.
With dreams held high and side by side
We gave life our token for one last ride
Arms in the air, at the top of our lungs
Together we screamed, "We're not done!"
Then we smiled and said, "This one's gonna be fun!"
My mother, my friend
My daughter, my twin
All my love, Lisa

My Third Born Son Ed

My third son, Eddie, has always been a nature lover. He wore cowboy boots every day from the first day he started walking. He was always hotter than everyone else in the room. He hated clothes as a toddler. When he was two years old, he was headed out the door naked to build a snowman. I told him he had to put on a coat and boots to go outside. I have a picture of him heading off the porch in just boots and an unbuttoned coat. He did have his hood pulled up, at least. I don't remember having to discipline him for anything. He was so easy to raise.

When he was four years old, he wandered around the meadow in farmers' coveralls, just being one with nature. He is our cuddly Koala Bear. This Animal Totem represents protection and a sense of security. Eddie's life has proved these traits follow him.

The family moved to California when Eddie was beginning junior high school. He decided he wanted to go by his middle name, Joseph. The whole family started calling him Joe. He never answered when we yelled, "Joe, Joe, Joe." Eventually, in a few weeks, we went back to calling him Eddie. He gave up the idea of being Joe.

We moved to another suburb of Los Angeles. When I was going to enroll Eddie in the new school, I had on a pumpkin suit with orange leggings because I was going to give a puppet show at his younger brother's elementary school. Eddie got a look of horror on his face and said, "You aren't going in that outfit, are you?" I answered frantically, "I have to! There isn't time to change before Patrick and Kevin's Halloween program."

Eddie sat down and refused to go until I finished their show and could change clothes. When I did take him into the high school office, all eyes were on us. Eddie is as handsome as a Greek God, and all the girls were whispering and pointing at the new student. I could see that the guys were looking suspiciously at Eddie.

A month later, he came home from school and said, "You have to get me out of that school! Those guys are going to kill me. All their girlfriends are making passes at me." I took him to the school counselor, and she agreed it was best to move him for his physical safety, mental clarity, and emotional peace of mind. They let him go to the other school in the area because we lived on the border of both schools.

He settled in this school and was content to finish high school. He came home the next year with a beautiful Polynesian girl on one hip and his surfboard on the other hip. I told him we were moving back to Ohio. Eddie got pale and replied in despair, "There is no surf there!" He didn't go with us. Instead, he moved in with his girlfriend. He graduated early and launched life as an adult. I wrote this when he moved out on his own at seventeen.

Aiming at the Stars

Aim at the Stars my dear one
Don't let fear overtake you, son
Set your dreams on high
Climb the stairway up to the sky
I hear you want magic
Don't let anything create static
Go for lightening your load
It requires an unencumbered road
Clear the channel to let in the light
Be humble in God's sight.
Clear your mind so spirit's messages you can hear
Be there for others, holding them most dear
Become a friend to one and all
Enjoy life and don't be afraid to fall
Then you can get so far
Perhaps you'll ride upon a Star

A Life Change for Eddie

When Eddie was in his mid-thirties, he was climbing a two-story contractor ladder. The ladder slid on wet tile and he crashed thirty feet to the ground, shattering both his heels and seriously injuring his back and hips. He told his younger brother, Kevin, "I just suddenly became an old man." I feel a Guardian Angel protected him and inspired me to write him a letter of encouragement:

Dear Eddie,

You are very precious to the Divine, and heaven honors you. Legions of Angels direct your path. What may seem like a tragedy is but a stillness to turn your life in the direction of your purpose on this earth. You came to teach lost souls that there is nothing that can overcome them unless they let it.

Remember, from whence you came, it is as vast as the cosmos. You are the starlight that everyone sees in the night sky. You are the shining sun at the break of day. All truth is within. Seek wisdom, and it will be revealed.

Find self-mastery through humility. Realize all your gifts and talents are given in trust to you for the benefit of the world. You have a special calling to serve humanity. Pray for God's Supreme power and wisdom to unfoldment in your life.

Ask for truth to be revealed, and so it shall be. Pray for the perfect place for you to do this work and for those who will assist in its manifestation. You will be given all that is needed to complete your ordained Earth Walk. Recall your youth and the connection you have with nature. You are truly One with all life.

Always I am with you and for you,
Your Mom

Eddie is an amazing survivor. He overcame all the limitations the doctors predicted. He has owned several businesses and is married to a wonderful, lovely lady named Cindy. She has been his inspiration, from their gorgeous wedding overlooking the California coast until now. She has two sons from her first marriage. Eddie has a daughter named Savannah from his first marriage.

Cindy and Ed bought a fabulous home in California. Eddie is still a surfer and an avid fisherman. He sold his coffee house business and is an author, real estate broker, and contractor, and helps his wife with her insurance agency. They travel the world sharing exotic places and delightful times. He no longer defines himself as old, even though he has had back issues again recently. Love truly blesses his path, and protection guides his life.

In his first book, *The Joy of Wealth* by Edward Longstreth (2011), he gives financial information but relates that true prosperity is the joy we find in financial security. His second book is a novel called *Wild Canyon*. It is full of information about the Old West. It keeps the reader on edge following exciting adventures from two periods of history.

My Fourth Born Son, Patrick

My son Patrick is one of those individuals that fortune smiles on. His older brother Trevor said, "Patrick has a 'blessed life." His Guardian Angel has certainly guided him from above because everything just worked out as a smashing success for him.

This is not without effort or exceptional talent on his part, but it helps to have providence working for us. Whenever I showed Patrick's picture to anyone as a baby, they said, "He looks like an angel, and you should have named him Gabriel." The Panda Bear is his Animal Totem. This represents luck and peace with gentleness and power.

We didn't get to take Patrick home from the hospital right away after his birth. He was treated for jaundice. The doctor told his father and me that they would have to do a full blood transfusion the next morning if his bilirubin count didn't go down. I prayed all night and called his Guardian Angel to help him. I saw Jesus over my tiny son's hospital crib that night. His bilirubin count went down, and in a few days, we were able to take him home to get to know his siblings.

Patrick was cuddled and adored by his three older brothers and sister. As an infant, his smile was only dimmed by his colic. There was just one thing that would console him when his tummy hurt. Patrick seemed to know the minute we walked outside, pushing him in his stroller. When the front wheels hit the front porch, he would stop screaming. The whole family took turns walking him during those nine months of colic. We circled the porch in bad weather and went around the block in good weather. We finally determined he was allergic to cow's milk. I drank milk while I was nursing.

We found he had outgrown this allergy in an interesting way. When he was about four, he asked me for a dog biscuit. I told him he couldn't have those and that they were only for our dog Cuddles. Patrick was always so grown up and logical in his reasoning. He intelligently related, "Eddie gives them to me." I loudly called his brother to the kitchen by his full name, "Edward Joseph Longstreth!" Eddie appeared quickly with a wide-eyed, deer-in-the-headlights look on his face. He knew he was in trouble.

Upon questioning Eddie, I found he and his friend had given Patrick dog biscuits from time to time as a joke. I found the box and read the label. They contained several of Patrick's allergy-sensitive foods. With tears of joy, I told Patrick he had outgrown his milk and wheat allergy. He thoughtfully requested, "Does that mean I can eat those biscuits?" I told him, "Of course not! Dog food is still not on your diet. Your brother is really in trouble for this." Ed spent a couple of hours in his room in timeout to think about the penalty of playing jokes at the expense of someone else.

When Patrick was nine years old, we moved to the Midwest, and his dad and I settled in Cincinnati with him and Kevin. My older offspring were grown, and each was on their own path. My marriage ended very soon thereafter. It was a tough decision, but we had grown apart, and life took us in different directions.

My Guardian Angel said it was in my highest good. It was also our sons' destiny to have two different backgrounds to broaden their life experience. I gave them a connection to nature, and their dad has given them the advantages of travel and education. There was always a deep love for them from both of us.

I moved to the backwoods near Bloomington, Indiana, and picked up my two youngest boys every weekend. We had all kinds of great adventures, from canoeing, survival training camp, and tube rafting to making decorations out of pinecones while we played in the woods. Their love of nature has remained an important part of their recreation and life experience. I cherish these times because they gave us a depth of knowing one another as friends, as well as mother and sons.

As I mentioned earlier, I moved to California in 1992 to help my oldest son, Brent, raise his three children when his wife died. Consequently,

I only got to see my sons three times a year. Patrick was ten, and Kevin was eight. They spent half the summer with me, Easter, and every other Christmas playing with their nieces and nephews. We collected shells at Seal Beach and rocks at Montano D'Or and played at the Butterfly Beach in Pismo. Whether playing Scrabble, Risk, Poker, or having a water balloon fight, Patrick's laughter and sense of humor are infectious.

Patrick's high school years were filled with golf, wrestling, and many friends. In college, his life of opportunity led him to England as a foreign exchange student. He made the best of it, traveling throughout Europe every weekend by train to Spain, Italy, and other surrounding countries. The first tours he told me about were trips to world-famous art galleries and golf courses.

He could always do what he set his mind to do. He looks so innocent. People trust him. He sold expensive knives door to door and didn't realize that selling over $4,000 in less than ten days was an incredible feat. His brother Trevor said, "If Pat can sell those, he can sell anything." Patrick had entrepreneurial qualities early in his career. He signed a national contract with Walmart and the orchid company he worked for during college.

He has always been artistically talented and majored in video graphics. After graduating from Washington University in St. Louis, MO, he got his Master's degree at Savannah College of Arts and Design. He started his career with a bang and used his creativity with a technical media company, making commercials and promotional videos. Patrick's talent, hard work ethic, and confidence got him a top-notch job as he moved up the ladder quickly.

He was the Visual Effects Supervisor of a television series and did special event coverage in Angeleselos. In his career, he contracted with Urban Redevelopment and City Planning, doing special projects in Savannah, GA. He traveled to Africa to do a documentary on environmental issues. He also traveled throughout Europe, demonstrating his graphic techniques. His favorite work is making films that help special needs individuals reach their goals.

My most cherished memories are the times I visited my adult children. I remember when Patrick phoned me saying he was eating alone at a Mexican restaurant in Washington, DC, and just wanted to visit. I got to enjoy his conversation with the waiter and the background noise as if I were there in person. It all seemed so surreal, as if I were at the table right beside him and wanted to order a margarita. It was such a good dinner conversation, relaxed and insightful, about our ideas on the world situation and family.

When Patrick calls me, he jokingly leaves a message saying, "This is Patrick, your favorite son." Well, all five of them are each my favorite sons, so he is right. Lisa is my favorite daughter, too. I have learned so much from him and his wonderful siblings. Patrick is the one to cheer up any group. A friend once asked him why he was so happy all the time. He answered, "I don't have anything to be unhappy about." What a great view of life!

Patrick is so helpful to others and has a kind, giving heart. I advised him not to overdo it like I had for so many years. He took on more than several people could get down in any time frame. I'd rather he is like me in other ways. It has been such a blessing to share his adventures. Patrick's name means Honored One, and that he is!

I wrote the following letter to Patrick during his Master of Arts Program.

Dear Patrick,

Sometimes, the desire to live life to the fullest and to fulfill everyone's expectations keeps a person from knowing what he/she wants in all that activity. Don't let life just go by while you are racing around. Most of the things a person fills their days with don't make them happy; they are only busy.

Please take time to live what is most important to you. When you get to the end of life and have no moments left, I hope you will have no regrets for the choices you made or for times lost for loving. Realize you can't turn the clock back and recapture what you lost along the way. Remember to live and enjoy the time you have.

My prayer for all my children is to take time to live the experiences and enjoy the cherished memories you can return to in reflection to warm your heart. I don't know who wrote it, but I've given this advice to many people, "Life is not measured by the number of breaths you take but by the moments that take your breath away."

Each one of your nieces and nephews has confided they are going through life junctures of re-evaluation. Please keep communication open with them so they will know their uncles are there for them in the conflicts of young adulthood. They need your friendship, your council, and faith in them. Remind them they are loved and respected and that someone is there for them. My sincerest intent has been to do this for you.

I love you,

Mama.

After graduating from college, Patrick got his Master of Arts in Savannah, Georgia. He met Anne at college, and they married in Savannah in an elegant southern-style mansion. Anne has been a yoga teacher, dancer, and graphic arts producer. To our surprise, she got my son to do a soft shoe dance at the wedding reception. Who would have thought? Patrick did say he was sweating the finale, hoping he would catch her as she fell back into his arms. Her trust in him paid off, for he did catch her. They have one of those marriages that are made in Heaven.

The Blessed Angel Falls to Earth

Life wasn't always a bowl of cherries for Patrick. He had a tendency to take on too much and try too hard to do everything to the ultimate. At age 32, this perfectionist found himself in a reality that failed to meet his expectations. He became overwhelmed with stress and back pain. He later learned the two were linked.

The pain made it impossible for him to sit down for more than an hour, and he left work on disability. Feeling lost and out of options, at the suggestion of a neurosurgeon, he received a high-dose steroid shot in his spine. The pain went away temporarily, but an allergic reaction to the steroids triggered a manic episode that landed him in a mental hospital for two weeks. Anne was with him all the way.

Patrick Tells His Story of Recovery

My recovery would not have been possible without the help of a good therapist and my devoted wife. Regular visits showed me a new way of understanding and processing my emotions. I had never thought to seek these tools in my adult life. Instead, I developed a bad habit of burying my emotional pain and frustration. Perfectionists have a hard time admitting they're not perfect, especially when it comes to their perfect brains.

Following this therapy, I returned to my usual life and work with a new outlook. I did my best to maintain a healthy diet and exercise. When it came to the mysterious back pain that started everything, I gave up looking for an explanation and chose to be grateful that it was at least manageable.

Anne and I had a picturesque wedding. Life was good! Two years after the initial episode, Anne came home with an amazing discovery. It was a news article about Dr. John Sarno, who had been curing patients with back pain for over forty years. He discovered a way to treat certain types of chronic pain with psychotherapy. When I read through his book *Healing Back Pain: The Mind-Body Connection* (John E. Sarno, M.D. 1991), I couldn't believe how accurately it described my condition.

Dr. Sarno was able to understand that many of the people coming to him did not suffer from misalignment, injury, or poor posture. Many doctors and chiropractors who fail to find the source in an X-ray or MRI will either give up or, worse, come to a faulty conclusion. The symptoms can sometimes be eased with massage therapy or painkillers, but the source is in the mind, and it can only be solved from there.

Upon finishing Dr. Sarno's book, my back pain got much worse for a couple of weeks. This is called the 'extinction burst.' It's a concept that applies to psychology, philosophy, and even sociology. When a new pattern of behavior is started, the subconscious mind will fight to maintain the order of doing things the way it knows.

Unlearning your pain is similar. When you realize that chronic pain is not the physical thing that you once thought it was, your brain will fight to prove you wrong. It will attempt to reaffirm the pain three-fold. But when that final extinction burst has passed, and the mind has conquered the brain and body, the pain simply evaporates. The prisoner is released from the vicious cycle.

Of course, no pain is ever gone forever. Scars remain, even the invisible ones. The best way to ensure it never comes back is to maintain a balanced life. Eating healthy is critical. I use exercise to release endorphins and burn off excess cortisol from stress. Most of all, I maintain a healthy mind. I can't let emotions fester. I don't let guilt eat me up. I keep a journal. Meditation helps me. I had to prioritize my life and be realistic with my goals. I learned the importance of taking care of the relationships that mean the most to me. As Bob Marley said, "Release yourselves from mental slavery; none but yourself can free your mind."

Summarizing Patrick and Anne's Impressive Accomplishments

Through all of this, his amazing wife, Anne, has been a loyal and supportive lifesaver. Their first child, Olive, was born on my dad's birthday. She is one year old now.

Resilience is a word that best describes our family. We just keep on keeping on when challenges come our way. Perseverance is what it takes to reach your goals. I hope these testimonials inspire others to never give up.

He excelled in his field and received notoriety for his short horror comedy film entitled "Hellyfish." The film was screened at many film festivals. Patrick and Annie produced a documentary about a young thirty-two-year-old woman with Down syndrome named Jasmine Faries. During the production of the play, we see Jazmine's struggle for independence and how a single spark of creativity can spread joy throughout a community. Patrick and Annie work to help others. They both stand for diversity and equality.

Their documentary entitled Iron Family won the Audience Award Fan Favorite at the Slamdance Festival and played at the famous Chinese Theater on Hollywood Blvd. Iron Family was also screened at the Dances with Films in Hollywood. The Barn's Fellowship gave Patrick and Anne a grant for their work on The Day That Shook Georgia about an industrial explosion. They continue to work on documentary films that bring recognition to those who give their all.

My Fifth Born Son, Kevin

I was in bed from the 6th week on during my pregnancy after a near miscarriage. We planned a natural home birth. I kept all the kids home to be a part of the sacred event the morning I went into labor. I couldn't reach the midwife or my husband. He had gone to work on an emergency. When they all finally got to our house, the midwife said we had to get to the hospital immediately. The baby's hands and feet were hanging out of the birth canal with the cord wrapped around the baby's neck. I had an emergency c-section about 15 minutes after we arrived at the hospital.

Kevin was the busiest child I have ever known. Keeping up with his curiosity and enthusiasm for activity was a challenge for my 41-year-old self. He brings joy and lifts the energy wherever he goes. I wrote the following poem for my youngest son. The Monkey Animal Totem describes Kevin as a toddler. I think his brothers and sister would agree he lives the Monkey's qualities of playfulness and curiosity.

Our wide-eyed wonder

Hair sticking straight up in the air
Throwing things asunder
There was nothing you wouldn't dare
A magnet of sheer energy and mirth
What a joy from morning to night!
Respecting others for their true worth
Lifting their lives with delight

This is a letter to Kevin in college when he was struggling with priorities.

Dear Kevin,

I am writing to you from the place of awareness in which we are truly One. It is very deep within my heart, and I have traveled to this remembrance of my role in your life. You have said for years you want to go to a third-world country to find meaning in life. Wherever you go, you will take yourself, your values, and your lifestyle with you.

Don't make your travels a quest for life answers, for they lie within your heart, your prayers, and in your journaling. You will only create busyness and escape from what is important unless you choose to prioritize inner stillness. You will eventually find that the wisdom was inside all the while you searched here and there. You will end up everywhere and still be nowhere. I hope you do travel to the four corners of the Earth. I fostered this spirit of adventure, and I honor your courage.

It doesn't matter if you are in South America, DC, or Hollywood; your heritage, family roots, true friends, spiritual rituals, and values are things to live and fight for. Truly, our world seems to be falling apart. All the decline of authority and integrity in our leadership is being exposed. This is the ordained point in our evolution for change and balance. I hope to be an inspiration to you and to all my children to be a part of bringing harmony within and without. This world we live in needs all of you, the Indigo and Star Children, for you are the hope of our future.

I love you,
Always your Mama

Another Letter to Kevin in College Written in his sophomore Year

To my Darling Monkey Kevin,
You are halfway there. Two years are completed, and two years are yet to go. I wonder where it will lead! I only know it will be stupendous! Savor the good times growing up. These include the quality adventures shared with Patrick, me, and the whole family. Laughing, playing, being! Hold our love close within as you face the upcoming times that beckon you into your life's destiny.

Kevin, may every encounter teach you more about yourself. Never hesitate to share the awareness gained with others as you move through the excitement of new discoveries. Delight in the simple pleasures of each day and find peace and guidance from the stillness within. My blessings are with you always as you continue to live in integrity.

Take care of yourself and remember I love you,
Your devoted Mama

Kevin's Graduation Day

Kevin graduated from George Washington University on the lawn of the White House with 900 students. I knew many of his friends, and it was a moving experience to witness the President address the student body. I wrote the following on Kevin's graduation card to inspire his destiny:

A Child Goes Forth

Son, honor your Higher Self, for this part of you takes care of your noble child within. Go into your heart to counsel with the higher part of yourself. Take the directions that this Divine part of you gives and see through the 'eye of love.' Your Guardian Angel speaks to you with this inner vision. Let it guide your path of leadership. The Star Ancestors and Ascended Masters await your entrance into the stillness with incredible multi-realm adventures. I am always with you heart to heart, supporting the rite of passage of your Earth mission as the child goes forth.

Your devoted Mama

Kevin excelled at everything he tried in his life. He started his career in high school at Dip and Dots Ice Cream in Cincinnati, OH. His sense of adventure took him on a quest all over the world. He backed packed around Europe. He worked as a tour guide on a whaleboat in Alaska. He ran jungle tours on the Amazon River in South America during the summer while in college. He and his fiancé set up a polo farm in Argentina.

He worked at a catering service in DC and then managed it after graduation from Georgetown University. They catered political events for over 2,000 people. He moved to Chicago for a job in department management at Four-Season Hotel. When he was filling out his resume for this career change a few years later, he asked me if he should put the last job on his resume. He was concerned it would make his experience look too diverse. I said, "Go for it. There was no way you can cover that up."

Kevin worked in account management for a national corporation for several years, and now he does large fundraising for a hospital in Chicago. He and a friend formed their own band in Chicago named Sponiband. The sky is the limit for him!

Kevin married his college sweetheart, Julie, in a unique, enchanting ceremony. Their relationship is what you read about in romance novels. They give each other space and yet are bonded in intimacy and modern liberated unity. He and Julie had baby Abe five years ago. What a red-hair delight, just like his father, always on the go! Now, they have a little red-haired baby girl named Jay Rocca. She already has her own voice in a big way! All my sons are quite active in raising their children and are involved in their care, as well as training values and guidelines.

My Greatest Acknowledgements in Life

As parents raise their families, you look at your original intentions and wonder how far short you have fallen to be everything you wanted to be as a role model. You question if you prepared your offspring for what challenges life will bring to them.

If you appreciate your parents, let them know. My children do. Words can be unmeasurable blessings. Here are some excerpts from letters that my family has written to me which mean more than I can express:

Dear Mama,

Thanks for bringing our entire wonderful family into the world and showing us how to share love and laughter. I hope you have a nice time with family and friends this Mother's Day. I miss you and am thinking of you as always.

Love from Patrick and Anne

Dear Mama,

I want to say thanks for being you and keeping me happy my entire life. I always loved you. Always! I love looking back at the insane number of laughs and fun we had. And still have!

Truly Yours,

Kevin

The following poems, written for me and framed as Christmas gifts, are great tributes to my goal to share quality time and values with my children:

My Mother
(Written by my son Eddie)
Where do I start, how can I say?
The strength of my appreciation I feel every day.
Was it the times shopping when you got me a Matchbox car?
Or the art class we took together just because of who you are?
Maybe you remember how you built me up,
With kisses and hugs, I was your koala pup.
Do you even fathom the depth of our together-time?
I respect you so much. I was your shadow, your mime.
So much of you in me, I am glad it is so.
You are the greatest mother that I will ever know.
Chakras, auras, the Stars, and the Sky.
Your wheatgrass and grapes taught me to be a man, not just a guy.
Your title and your job as a mother were clear,
To raise your children to be self-sufficient and sincere.
You took it so much farther, way beyond what was expected.
You opened my mind and my heart even when I sometimes objected.
Weekends of affirmations, dream building, and acupressure,
There are no other kids in the world who know such pleasure.
I am so proud of my childhood, I experienced so much love,
Of kindness and creativity, you inspired from above.
Now that I am older, grown in my own way,
I still call to you for your wisdom to color my gray.
Time has passed and I wanted to elaborate,
You are the best Mother in the world, respected and great.

While Kevin and Patrick were in college, they sent me a framed poem. Kevin wrote the poem entitled "Thank You for All the Memories." Patrick made a composite picture of happy times shared as they were growing up. The picture has a white dove superimposed across it.

I am excited to share more information about the younger generation in our family if you will indulge me. I have learned more from the relationships with those I love than from any other experiences. Praying to be the person they need has challenged me to grow. Their love and respect motivated me to find a higher meaning in life and have been the stimulus to find the best of myself.

CHAPTER THIRTEEN
ENJOYING MY GRANDCHILDREN

I know why they call your children's children 'grandchildren.' Mine are amazing. Just ask me about them if you have all day.

I wanted to be called some cute name, but my oldest granddaughter, Tara, named me plain old Grandma. It stuck with all the grandchildren, except Cory, who calls me his Grams, and Abe, who calls me Grandmama. I think we are going to stick with that name while Ava, Leah, Natalie, and Brently grow up. They are great-grandchildren, but that is the next chapter.

To My First Grandchild

Tara: Fire Unleashed

What a sweetheart
A red-haired ball of fire
I was so sad when we had to part
I pray someday she fulfills her desire
A precious doll from the start
Fairest of the Los Angles Fair
She already was at three
Drawing her art to share
Her spirit must be free

Advice to Tara

The following is advice to my oldest granddaughter, Tara, when she graduated from high school:

Go somewhere with a decision to move forward, rather than just leaving the place you have been. Let your future guide you from within. Be strong, firm, and forthright in choices to support your own 'greater good'. May you always allow destiny to lead you into its awakening. Remember what a blessing you are.

Take care of yourself.

Always loving you,

Grandma

Anorexia and Us

My granddaughter Tara had the classic symptoms of anorexia. This became another big hurdle to face. It is a disease grounded in dysfunctional thoughts and distorted body image. I saw all these patterns manifest in my own family when she was diagnosed with anorexia at sixteen.

Several changes in our family resulted in my granddaughter feeling that she had no control over her life. I moved to Ojai, CA, after living with my son for several years. If I had stayed in the Pismo Beach area, it would have been a smoother transition for the children when I left their home, but my work called me elsewhere.

A new stepmother and stepsister brought adjustments for Brent's three children. New family rules and family members to please created a challenge for Tara. She seemed to lose control as all regular daily chore schedules, meals, bedtime rituals, family outings, and décor changed. Tara later related to me that what she ate was one of the only things she could control.

Her tendency to be shy was based on insecurity. Feelings of not being good enough can lead to unhealthy eating patterns. When this cycle excelled, it added to the low self-esteem and increased the lack of self-control that she was experiencing. Tara said she was told that she had big bones and was warned before first grade that she had to be careful not to get fat. I certainly didn't tell her that!

Anorexics have a distorted body image and believe they are fat no matter how thin they get until they die of starvation. The anorexic feels safe and in control only when their stomach is empty. Bulimia is often a part of the pattern of dysfunctional attitudes regarding food. This was true of my granddaughter. Bulimics eat and make themselves throw up to get rid of the food they feel is going to destroy their hope for acceptance. Since they throw up food, they are continuously hungry and vitamin deficient. Many health problems result in digestion and absorption.

An intense desire to please is transferred into false self-worth. Tara said she got a sense of pride for going without food longer than other people. Eventually, this illusionary superior status based on inferiority creates a withdrawal from outside activities. A preoccupation with dieting takes over. The individual can become so nutrient-depleted that they don't think clearly or lead a normal social and school life. If eating becomes an obsession, as it does in anorexia, friends, family, and school become less and less important.

Watching the food channel on television became my granddaughter's main pass time. I remember Tara was so mad about getting a cookbook on pastry for her birthday. She asked for recipes on the preparation of fancy salads, not this book on sweets. She was preoccupied with her stepmother's opinion of her, as well as her peers. I had tried to teach her to have self-worth, but it hadn't worked. Loving her had not been enough!

Tara was always so sweet and likable. All her teachers had told me she was a delight to have in their class and was so quiet. They asked if she talked more at home. Tara confided in me and relaxed when we were together. I wondered if she would ever do this again after I moved away. I worried that trust had been broken and feared we couldn't ever go back to the confidence shared after the family crisis of her anorexia. This fear was unfounded, for we have a great level of communication regularly now.

My granddaughter was losing weight at an alarming rate. She lost forty-five pounds and weighed just over eighty in high school. When I went to visit them, my son was trying to encourage ice cream and other fattening foods, as well as more meat and potatoes. Tara was wearing large baggy clothes. She confided in me that she was throwing food away and had stopped her period three months previously. Thick peach fuzz had started growing on her arms in the body's attempt to stay warm. She exercised constantly on a treadmill while watching the food shows alone in her bedroom.

In the book *Straight Talk About Eating Disorders*, Maloney and Kranz (1991) discuss the pattern of fear. They relate that the anorexic girl is afraid to stop exercising for fear that the little food she has eaten will turn to fat. The anorexic has lost touch with her hunger and may binge and purge. Many anorexics are relieved to feel hunger because this means they aren't gaining weight. They only feel safe when they have an empty stomach. My granddaughter fit this pattern. Tara seemed to be afraid to be at rest and was tormented by thoughts of being unacceptable. She was in constant motion.

In *The Golden Cage*, Hilde Bruch explains that distorted feelings about the body and its function can develop in longer-term anorexia. The anorexic individual often has feelings of not measuring up to their siblings or friends. They fear judgment, especially from their parents and other authority figures.

While visiting my son's new family in Arroyo Grande, CA, Tara and I were talking in their tree cove in the backyard. She confided some alarming information about her eating habits. She knew just how many times she had to chew before she allowed herself to swallow. This number was seventy-seven. She cut her food into tiny bites, drank large amounts of water between bites, and counted every gram of fat. In unrealistic comparisons to others, Tara believed she was the ugly duckling.

I noted her symptoms of dizziness, loss of concentration, irritability, depression, bruises, sunken eyes, pale skin tone, and a low tolerance for cold temperatures. Tara said she was most concerned about her thinning hair. Her beautiful copper-red hair was falling out by the handfuls. It had previously tumbled in ringlets of thick curls.

My son asked me to take her to the doctor stating I was the only one she would listen to. She was so thin the whole family was getting worried. He was alarmed when he got the call to meet us at once in the emergency room. He said he'd come right away and bring his new wife. I saw my granddaughter's little frame tense up as the nurse said they would both be there as soon as possible. The doctor also noted her reaction and said for Brent to come alone. Tara didn't want to look bad to the stepmom whom she wanted to impress. In the initial examination, medical tests confirmed low blood pressure, irregular heart rhythms, and numbness of the soles of her feet.

The doctor took EKG readings every fifteen minutes and then sent my granddaughter, by ambulance five hours up the coast to Stanford Medical Center. It is a world-renowned clinic for eating disorders. We took two cars trailing behind the ambulance to San Francisco. The doctor at the Stanford Medical Clinic came in and asked for a private conference on her declining condition. The doctor informed Brent and me that her heart could stop at any time because it was so weak.

The hospital staff would not permit my granddaughter to walk to the bathroom or digest solid food, as this was too great a strain on her emancipated eighty-five-pound body. The doctor said she would need all her strength to heal and might have permanent heart damage. She was on intravenous feeding and then only liquids after a few days.

They began putting her in a warming bed at night because her body temperature was dropping to an alarmingly low rate during sleep. I sat beside her skeletal form in the hospital. Trying to be jovial through my tears, I said, "Well, at least we know you don't have big bones!" She was too weak to laugh.

The doctor said he didn't know how long she would have to stay in the Anorexic Clinic. I drove down the coast alone and remember wailing most of the way back in agony that I was losing my beloved grandchild. Upon my return to Arroyo Grande, I sat and cried for hours on the sands of Butterfly Beach, pouring my tears into Mother Earth. I prayed and did a ceremony to release family karma. I sent light energy and reiki. Then, I gave her to Divine in the circle of trees where the ocean meets the forest on the dunes near Pismo Beach. I had just brought my granddaughter to this circle of trees to do a rite of passage ritual for her sixteenth birthday, the week before going to the doctor's office.

She now felt I had betrayed her by taking her to the hospital where she would be forced to eat and gain weight. This didn't happen after all because the doctor said the digestion process would take too much of her life force. Tara was being fed intravenously and given two liquid meals daily. They released Tara into a continued care program in Arroyo Grande after a few weeks.

In *The Golden Cage*, Hilde Bruch MD explains that the anorexic feels inadequate and judged by others. Therapy must help them understand this erroneous thinking. Behavior can be modified in several ways. Two effective ones are self-hypnosis and Neuro-Linguistic Programming (NLP). Tara responded very positively to the use of these therapies to recreate stable supportive childhood experiences, that rebuilt her self-esteem. I took time off my job to help in her recovery. It took several kinds of intervention. A weekly counselor talked to the whole family in a series of sessions to address underlying causes and emotional issues.

The counselor aided in changing my granddaughter's relationship to my son's nuclear family. She began to learn her place in this new family unit. She got vitamins, dental, gynecological hormone treatment, NLP., and consultations with a nutritionist. Her recovery was found through the process of improved mind, body, and spiritual health. She learned to love herself more and to stop making comparisons to others. I could see there was progress as Tara accepted her worth through our talks.

One of the biggest factors in her recovery was that she came to live with me during her senior year in Columbus, OH. As her self-confidence was restored, we progressed to sort through some different attitudes about her life direction. She was influenced by my more casual approach to eating and body image. I began to eat healthier foods, so we helped one another and enhanced our loving bond.

One of my happiest memories was when Tara experienced snowflakes for the first time when I was driving her to school that winter morning. She rolled down the window and held out her hand to capture the flakes in midair. I'll always cherish the look of wonder on her face. We said nothing but just reveled in the glory of the moment.

Tara graduated high school and went to college in Mississippi, where her other grandparents lived. A couple of years after that, she was considering a career in modeling, being a chef, or airline stewardess. Tara's recovery was found through the process of improved mind, body, and spiritual health.

Spirituality was an important factor in her recovery through an integrative health process. A person must come to a place of self-acceptance. Unconditional love is the answer to the personal and family dynamics involved in the judgmental and control issues that are born out of insecurity. When she was twenty, I talked to her about how she felt four years earlier in the grip of anorexia. Here is her response:

Tara Tells About Her Anorexic World

At sixteen, it was easy for me to feel unattractive, comparing myself to a model. I had feelings of not being good enough. A good day was when I stuck to my diet and a bad day was when I ate something that I wasn't supposed to. Food became a way to avoid other issues in my life. I felt safe only when my stomach was empty. By controlling my body, I could control the bad feelings that I wasn't allowing myself to express. I thought I had to count every gram of fat and I ate tiny bites. Then Dad would think I was eating more. My sense of importance was centered around being thin and noticed by Dad.

In more recent conversations, I spoke with her regarding the issue of anorexia. She looked off into the distance and spoke quietly as if remembering her lessons. She said, "I had to change the circumstances of my life to get well. It's harder to control one's life than to stay anorexic. Many people never can make all the necessary changes. Sometimes a person holds so much anger at others, they don't eat to make them worried. I decided to be happy and go on with my life instead."

Tara Moves On

Her father and I were talking on my visit to California, in June 2007. We agreed that Tara had found her autonomy and was constructively controlling her own life. Finally growing up in her own right meant standing up and being her unique adult self. Her individualization is now the guiding force in her personality. Self-love was the key to her freedom. Harmony and joy became the theme of her life story.

I couldn't help but remember the pain I felt when I thought we were losing Tara in her teen years. This was replaced by the exalted joy that I felt at Tara's wedding. As a licensed minister I could legally perform her wedding to Gary, in Moss Point in August 2019. Her father Brent had a stroke a few months earlier. He had recovered enough to fly in from California, to give his eldest daughter's hand to her new husband. Several of our family members were able to attend and share their blessings. I feel the promises Gary and Tara made to one another in their vows can keep marriage exciting and anew through the years to come.

Tara and Gary's Wedding Vows August 3, 2019

Grandma: May each of you bring the best of yourselves to this marriage.

May you treat yourself and each other with kindness and guidance, protection and nurturing.

Tara and Gary, do you want to share these qualities of love and to the best of your abilities enjoy the peace this provides?

The couple replies together: Yes, we do.

My Second Granddaughter Heather Feather (Her nickname)

Heather was born in Huntington Beach, CA. Oct of 1986. She has been beautiful all of her busy life. She crawled, walked, and talked early. I went over once a week to give my daughter-in-law a day out. I took my two granddaughters to the park, got ice cream, and went to festivals.

Always on the go, Heather was fearless playing soccer in elementary school. She ran for the ball ahead of the whole team and drove in the goals. She was like a one-person dynamo. Her dream was to be a doctor and her intelligence would have enabled her to do that. She fell in love with a semi-pro baseball player in college. They married and started a family instead. She did just as I had done, gave up college for what seemed like love.

Child of the Stars

I wrote this letter to Heather in her second year of college:

Dear Heather Feather,
Set your sites high to determine where you are
Seeking to reach the potential of your dreams
For you can truly go far
Don't let anyone get in the way of your schemes
Two beautiful baby daughters you have birthed into our family
What a task you have undertaken to raise them alone
Continue to follow your heart to reach your destiny
From the busy child, a mature woman has grown

Always stand up for what you believe and what is important to you. There will be battles in life, and you will need to decide what is worth fighting for, and what isn't. You will need to know when to take a stand and when to let it go. If it is time for a change, let go of what has been and what will be.

Challenges are opportunities to get through the bases; first, second, third, and on into home base. When the going is rough, ask yourself what little gemstone you got from the situation. I have faith that you will make your life count and will be an inspiration to others.

Love from your Grandma

Women's Drumming Ritual

While living with my son Brent, I taught my young granddaughters about women's rituals, totem animals, and their personal power. We went to a Native American drumming circle with forty other women up the coast in Montano D' Orr and dressed in long skirts because this was part of the ritual of respect. We ate out and walked on the beach gathering rocks and shells. I still have some of the small rocks that had holes in them worn by the movement of the tide. Heather called them Holy Stones.

Tree Cove Ritual with My Two Oldest Granddaughters

I had a vision of a women's ceremony I was to do with my granddaughters. I awaken them early before school to catch the Moon cycle energy. We went to the Tree Cove in the back of my son's home and walked the circle from left to right. We called in the Guardians of the Directions and gave prayers of gratitude.

My younger granddaughter, Heather, brought a rosebud to use in the ritual. We put it in a small glass turned upside down. This would represent the enclosed space we may sometimes choose to live in, instead of facing bigger and better opportunities. I encouraged them to avoid the limitations life can present. My older granddaughter, Tara had found a small piece of wood to represent the wisdom of the Trees and Nature Spirits. She said," It wants to be in our ceremony."

We shook our rattles to loosen the harmful energy in the ethers and began a ritual to end the need for violence in ourselves and within the Earth. The girls rattled and drummed. They added their sounds that seemed to come from the Earth Mother herself. We danced around the circle for cleansing and clarity. Then we burned a piece of paper with the word 'war' written on it. We took the rose out of the ball jar, proclaiming triumph over all acts of violence and suppression.

We watched the paper burn, drummed and rattled over it, and then buried the ashes. The very second that we finished our ritual, drops of rain fell right in the center of the circle. The drops only fell in this one place. Heather said, "Oh look! Great Spirit has blessed our ritual and honors us."

Out of the mouths of babes, we find wisdom.

Coming of Age Passage Rite Ritual

Each of my three granddaughters went with me privately to the tree cove on Pismo Beach to do their women's rite of passage ritual. This special ceremony was conducted in a circle of welcoming Eucalyptus Trees. I felt each time we entered this sacred space, we were to ask the Tree that formed an arch if we could enter the cove. We waited briefly for an answer of acknowledgment and began the welcoming of womanhood with songs of honor to the Earth Mother and drumming. My granddaughters then made a promise to the Great Spirit to live in integrity and make wise choices.

I have equated birds as Animal Totems for my granddaughters. With her red hair, Tara's Totem is the Cardinal. I have heard, "If a Cardinal appears, Angels are near." Tara is our mythical Mermaid sharing magic with us through her art. I relate the Phoenix Bird to Heather. When they were little, I called her Heather Feather. It is about resilience and new beginnings. Eddie's daughter, Savannah and I share the Animal Bird Totem of the Dove for hope.

My Third Granddaughter Savannah
Our Connection

Savannah and I share a birthday only three days apart. We always find a special something to get both of us alike, in the shops along the coast; a stone, a necklace, or whatever takes our fancy. Once when we were on a shopping trip during my California visit, we found a compact with a mirror for face powder. It says, "Be You Always." It is our bond through time and expresses what I have struggled to be throughout my life. It is the little things that are the most important. My grandchildren are never far from me.

The last time I visited California, we went to an art gallery in Cambria. I fell in love with this sculptured purple heart with a Dove which had the saying, "May your heartbeat with the rhythm of hope." Since 'hope' is one of my mantras, Savanah got the sculpture for me and surprised me with it at lunch. What a sweet, caring person she is!

Savannah is forging on with her education. Although she has had several changes in her career goals, she has stayed true to the love of her life Otis. They share a lovely home in California near her father.

Savannah: The Charmer

"S" is for selfless, a generous soul.

"A" is for affectionate, a heart of gold.

"V" is for virtues, an angel's heart.

"A" is for achiever, so talented and smart.

"N" is for noble, kind little princess.

"N" is for naturally sweet, hugs and kisses.

"A" is for adorable, gift from above.

"H" is for happy, so precious, and loved.

My Oldest Grandson Cory

I have felt that Cory and my other and all my children have special callings. These children are aware of the power within. At two years old, Cory had gifts of healing and foresight which may be revealed as he gets older. Many of the children born after 1998 were indigos or crystal children. They are thought to have more advanced DNA and better function of both the left and right brain.

These sensitive beings question authority and have solutions for the New World. They seem to also have precognition. Ancient prophecies tell of these special children and encourage us to listen to their wisdom. I read in Bible studies, "A little child shall lead them. Except you become as a little child, ye shall not enter the kingdom of heaven."

My grandson Cory has been one of my biggest teachers of mystical law. My daughter Lisa had him very young in 1986. I was the first person who got to hold him after he entered this Earth plane as Lisa's birth attendant. Lisa had a c-section and the delivery doctor handed him to me while he finished her surgery. He started out the hard way then and kept right on with this approach to life. Cory talked early and walked early. He was much smaller than his years but much wiser. We decorated his whole nursery room with Bears and I call him our Cory Bear. This Animal Totem represents qualities of loyalty, strength, and introspection.

Cory never seemed like a baby even in his crib days. I would sense his frustration that he wanted to walk across the room and couldn't understand why he wasn't able to do this. He didn't want to waste time crawling. It was like he remembered being mobile in a past life and couldn't understand why he had to be an inept baby again. He remembered things in preschool about other life experiences and related happenings about his future. He has been mystical and advanced for his age his whole life.

Cory is one of the most powerful men I have been blessed to have the honor of helping to raise. Keeping up with Cory was always a challenge. One day we had to take Cory to the emergency room twice. He fell into a friend's hot tub and Lisa did CPR to save him until the paramedics could get there. Later that same day, we had to return to the hospital with him screaming because a string from the carpet was wound so tightly around his toe that we couldn't get it off. It had to be surgically cut by the physician.

The next morning, he was sitting at the kitchen table eating cocoa puffs. Seeing the worried, frazzled look on my face, Corry excitedly declared, "Don't worry about me Grams. Someday I will start vibrating faster and faster and I'll turn into purple light." He threw his arms up and out to each side exclaiming, "It will be wonderful and then I can see you from everywhere." Cory's first twenty-one years were tumultuous, but success waits just around the corner for him and his Guardian Angel is always nearby. I have heard the saying, "Who knows what magic tomorrow may bring?"

Our Cross Country Journey

Cory and I were going on a journey from Cincinnati to California, for Christmas in 1991. I still have perceptual disturbances and get lost easily. Directions have always been a challenge for me. Hopelessly looking for the post office in Cincinnati, before we left brought nagging pain in my Solar Plexus. Cory asked his mother Lisa, "How will Grams ever find her way to California when she gets lost trying to mail a letter in this town?"

Lisa responded, "Just keep telling her to follow the compass Eddie gave her when he was six and go West." I listened to Cory, and we barely made it in time for the traditional Christmas Eve Candle-lighting Ritual at his uncle Brent's in Arroyo Grande, California. We had a great visit with the family that holiday.

On the return trip, I seemed to forget it was winter all over the USA except sunny California. We took the northern route back to Cincinnati through Vale, Colorado. There were warnings that only those vehicles with chains and snow tires were legal on the roadways. I had neither, but we forged on. What could we do? We were there in a blizzard. There were no motels in sight. At one point it was blowing snow and was so foggy that I had zero visibility. We slid back and forth careering across the highway lanes and ended up temporarily stranded in a snow drift on the side of the road. If we had gone to the left, we'd have slid off the side of the mountaintop.

Cory asked me if we were going to die. He was only four and had already faced death through the perils of my driving. I told him we had survived the camping trip through six states, for six weeks, with all six kids. I knew our Guardian Angels were with us then, and they were also with us on this journey. We made it home safe and sound.

Cory had another close call when he was a little older when we were hunting shells on the California beach. The tide came in and nearly swept Cory out into the ocean. His uncle Kevin barely grabbed his hand to rescue Cory from dashing against the rock wall in the cave we were in, seeking refuge from the rising tide water. I wrote this about my adorable grandson Cory:

Cory's Rite of Passage Ritual.

Imp -Angel Boy- Teacher – Friend
Light of our lives
Yes, you have always been
Always figuring a way
Getting 'this' done
Doing what others don't even see
Loyal son
Guided by your destiny

Our respect you have won
I know you'll find your place
Growing up before most should
Sharing strength with a brave face
Crossing the threshold of adulthood
Going within to discover the truth for yourself
Mystic leader, your Grams knew
You'd show the world the meaning of wealth
For at a young age, you'd learned the value of love
Heaven sent you – our cuddly bear, our little man
With your mother's guidance and gifts from above
Adversity brought you to reveal a bigger plan

Cory came to live with me in 2008. I was having a rough time during my return to college after a marriage breakup. I had been a recluse studying for my master's degree and trying to integrate the lessons of my last marriage. My family was worried about my declining health. I became more secluded and was dealing with skin cancer which caused scabs and lesions all over my face. I found a level of insecurity I had never experienced.

Cory said he hardly recognized me. His faith in me encouraged me to take care of myself by enjoying the present moment. He helped me remember what is truly important in life. I decided to focus on where I was going with my educational process. I vowed to reach out to others and be my old self in an improved way. Restorative treatments finally cleared the sores leaving no facial scars.

Appreciation of Cory

Cory is a loyal friend to those he loves. He is a life adventurer. At age twenty-nine, Cory was swimming with the dolphins in the Virgin Islands. He got very sick and the hospital there wanted to airlift him to Cuba. That was the only hospital that could deal with his kidney failure. My daughter got him a flight the next morning, to Cincinnati to University Hospital. After getting him up to his room, he held my hand and said weakly, "I don't think I'm going to make it through, Grams."

After two weeks and a close brush with death, he and his mom came to live with me at my retreat center located in the woods of Kentucky. Cory learned to honor his life while on dialysis for nine months. Miraculously, he was taken off dialysis and got a full-time job as a dealer in a casino. He faced death and then had to face life. I know he will find his way. I respect he has always been so insightful and tells it like it is. We shared Thanksgiving that year at my daughter's cabin in the woods. Cory has what it takes to make his life plans work. He followed his dreams in a brave move to California.

My Grandson Matthew: The Teacher

I wrote this when I was co-parenting Matthew with Brent after his mom died in 1990 when he was two years old.

> We tried to show you how much we cared
> Maybe you'll understand the times shared
> When your dad and I were just trying to teach you to be a man
> You have been our Peter Pan
> While existing in the world of lost boys
> Games and fun were your ploys
> The time you did span
> While we had another plan
> Someday you'll find your true place in adult life
> Know it is a journey worth the strife
> I have faith you'll discover love
> Know it is there for you with blessings from above

Matthew was a six-month preemie. He survived weighing just over two pounds. As a toddler, he fell and hit his head on a rock. He was climbing a hill by the lake with his dad. At two years old, Matthew developed cataracts from these traumas. He was only able to see shadows and was diagnosed as clinically blind. The doctor said he needed surgery to have his lenses removed. He would have to wear glasses until later in his teens when his eyes were fully developed and big enough to implant permanent lenses.

Matthew was often forgetful as a young child. He had little awareness of special relationships and little respect for boundaries. He began to demonstrate a split personality in school. He had been through a traumatic five years with his mother's death and his eye surgery. Mathew was very accident-prone and occasionally didn't seem to be tuned into his surroundings.

When Matthew was a small child, I asked him to work with me to listen more carefully. He agreed to try. The emphasis was to be in the moment, concentrating on safety and consideration of his and other's property. I developed exercises to teach this after getting his cooperation.

He practiced riding his bike and skating, noticing what was going on around him to avoid an accident. He was to think about each thing he was doing as he did it. His goal was to completely focus on that exact task. This might be doing a chore, eating, brushing his teeth, or walking to school. Previously, Matthew had been too busy playing and finding excitement without connecting where he was. He gradually became more focused and did better in school. He has a genius IQ and developed a computer program for the Montessori school he attended.

Matthew is a man now and has many magical qualities. He lives in worlds of Dragons, rap music, and adventures. He has a delightful outlook on life. He laughs at the humor of life's daily ebb and flow. Daily challenges don't seem to bother him in ways they do lots of people. I always appreciate it when he calls just to talk.

Matthew and I connect with Dragons and Wolves. We send each other colorful pictures that I frame and put in my Crystal Sanctuary meditation room. The Wolf is Matthew's Animal Totem and represents the teacher. Matthew is truly another one of my important teachers. He too seems to have secrets of living we all need to learn. Dragons teach us we are powerful and can do anything we want.

Matthew is quite talented musically and is the rapper Lil Causser.

My Precious Grandsons Dylan and Elliott:
The Playful Elves

Their father, Trevor was almost fifty when he had these darling little guys. On my 75th birthday, I visited them on the California coast when Dylan was four and Elliott was one. It brought back memories of their father so many years ago. He carried both of his little boys on his back just like he did his younger brothers, Patrick and Kevin when he was a teenager and they were his son's age. Life is really a circle!

Both Trevor and Lisa regularly play with Dylan and Elliott. They are getting such creative stimulation. I enjoyed working puzzles, playing hide and seek, watching cartoons, coloring pictures, and building all kinds of structures with their blocks. Their mom, Lisa, took the boys and me to story time at the library and a music class for toddlers. It was Elliott's first birthday. What a party! The catered event had a blow-up wading pool and slide for the young children. The Animal Totem of the playful energetic Puppy represents Dylan and Elliott. The Dog Totem relates to abundant energy and loyalty.

Dylan uses his lawn mower just like he saw the gardeners. The day before the party he wouldn't let me sit down until I made a couple of rounds around the entire yard with his toy mower. Then he said, "No sitting yet; we aren't done." He is just like his father, a real go-getter. Dylan has a heart of gold and looks like his mother and dad. He is an adorable busy bee.

Elliott is the image of Trevor's baby pictures. He is a cuddle bug like his dad was. What a charmer, and he loves mealtime and the outdoors. I got to see his first independent steps. He took a few steps and then was running before the week was out. It wasn't long before he was going constantly and running his parents ragged.

Dylan – the Peacemaker

Determined from the start
You are coming out to make your mark
As you get older, others will see
What a leader you can be

You protect and defend
Helping those in need to the end
Running the clock past time
You never stop until solutions you find

You keep at it and don't ever waver
From the answers that must be savored
Hopefully, you let others help you in your plight
As you give each task all your might

You are a get-it-done-guy
Kind and caring up to the sky
Fun and fantasy your quest
Always giving it your best

Elliott- the Troubadour

Lively and filled with rhythm and dance
Your fancy-free spirit moves at every chance
When night falls and day is done
You still shine the light of the sun

Setting the pace for others to grow
Virtues of love you do show
Enjoying the best of you and the best of me
We'll discover how to be free

Always the hero, singing in times of strife
Lifting fear to find a deeper meaning in life
Giving your sweet smiles so kind
To bring forth what we all seek to find

Traveling on the path of peace and joy
You'll forever be our precious boy
The Stars will reveal what your future brings
As you teach us to delight in magical things

A Blanket for Baby Abe

Before Abe was born, I decided to sew a satin border on the new blanket I just got for him. It turned into quite an adventure. I had not even opened my sewing machine in 30 years. Since it was Mother's, it felt like something I should keep. I had moved it from place to place and now I knew why. I was supposed to bind my grandson's blanket with it. I began by being thrilled that I remembered how to thread the machine. I started with a positive attitude to bind the small bib-size blanket instead of a full body-size blanket.

This project became a life review that was composed of all my hang-ups and lessons. It was a walk-through time. I set the objective to make this blanket special. I heard the words inside my head, "I want this to be perfect". The first few stitches went smoothly. Well, this should be a breeze, I thought. Those were the last stitches that were easy. The thread snarled, and I snarled! I got that straightened out and reminded myself I was putting only positive energy into little Abe's tiny blanket. I visualized it filled with love to comfort him. The satin edge could be calming to him.

His father Kevin had loved a satin night gown that I wore when he was a baby. He sucked his thumb and rubbed my satin sleeve between his fingers. It was the only time Kevin was still. I said to myself, I wonder if Abe will like this. I wonder if Kevin and Julie will like it. I laughed with amusement that I was still wondering what 'they' would think. I rounded the first corner, no problem. Whoops!

The white binding had slipped and was sewed in place lopsided. I realized I was holding my breath. Then I remembered years of ripping out seams due to my dyslexia. This thought almost brought tears. There was no need to rip out the stitches. Cutting off the extra white satin binding would make it look like it was even. I was clenching my teeth and stressing, and needed to focus.

I made another mistake on the next corner. Oh no! I can't do this! Then I corrected this old belief and took a deep breath of the all-important oxygen. I felt proud of myself for replacing this failure pattern and releasing the 'inept' programming of my childhood. Good times that were connected to Mother's sewing machine began to come to mind.

Making clothes for my granddaughter's stuffed toys years earlier was a happy memory.

I sewed matching pant suits for Patrick and Kevin when they were little and made plaid shorts for them and their teenage brothers when we moved to California. They looked so cute with all four of them alike. Trevor and Eddie wouldn't leave the house if any of them were wearing these matching shorts the same day.

Mother made my clothes on this same sewing machine. I loved the dotted-swiss sundress and petticoats with lots of ruffles. I especially liked the cowgirl outfit with a jacket she made me for school. Mother made most of my clothes including my poodle skirt. She also made an Indian dress with fringe for the school play, a pioneer costume, and a strapless formal for the Cotillion dance. This sewing machine truly touched the lives of several generations in our family.

I started having reversals and sewing things backward just like I did while growing up in school. I thought, 'I can't do this." Suddenly, I felt like the little engine that could. I said over and over, "I think I can. I think I can." I stopped and laughed about the encouragement this children's book was giving me. I had been all over the ladder up and down with doubt and renewed faith.

I finished the last side and surveyed the finished product. Well, it wasn't perfect, but it was perfectly fine. The tiny blanket with white binding certainly had lots of love.

I put up my mother's portable sewing machine and took it to the garage where my moving sale was set up. I happily resolved that Abe's tiny blanket would be my last sewing project with my mother's machine. I ended up giving it to my friend because I couldn't sell this treasured family relic after all.

Abe was born in October 2017 on his Uncle Eddie's birthday. He weighed 7 lbs. 10 ounces. I hoped he'd like his blanket. I wrote him the following letter.

Dear Abe,

You are only a few hours old now. Your dad, Kevin, asked me to be the communication source to the family when your mom went into labor. I wrote the following poem while counting the minutes until your birth. You will bring joy and thanksgiving untold to our family and others as time goes by.

Today the whole family awaited your arrival
Now you're the main reason for your parent's survival
We gifted you with wild celebration our bundle of love
You are born in a world in need of hope from the dove
We know you will be a blessing to all and enjoy your life
For your generation is coming to end struggle and strife
What does the future hold for you dear Baby Abe?
I wonder what joy is yours to be made!

Abe Rocky Garfield's Ceremony of Dedication Nov. 22, 2017 Officiated by Grandmama, Reverend Patrice Joy

Abe's Christening was very similar to the one given to each child born in our family. All the family members give a blessing. It is a dedication from our whole family to raise the child in loving support and respect for their heritage.

I do not know the authors who wrote the blessings that are read by our family members. Some were original. These are writings that have touched my heart.

The Dedication Service

We are here to share in the love and joy this new baby boy has brought to our family. We want to be aware of the Divine's guidance in the years before us. Let us always express unconditional love in our hearts and our homes. As we explore how to do this, I'd like to look at the parent's role in raising a child.

What shall we give our children?
Give them more patience, a kinder sympathetic ear,
a little extra time for laughter, or tenderly drying a tear.
Take time to teach them the fulfillment of doing a task.
Find time to answer more of the questions they ask.
Read books together and take long walks in the sun.

Make time for a bedtime story after the day is done.
Giving these to your child weaves a close tie,
knitting your lives together with gifts that money can't buy.

Kevin and Julie will now offer their prayer intention and gratitude for Abe.

Mama and Papa's Prayer Intention of Gratitude

Thank you for this new baby in our family and for all the joy he is bringing to our home. We ask for your guidance in raising Abe. Help us be worthy of the trust in those shining eyes and the expectations in his little heart. We ask his Guardian Angel to give us the wisdom to love without over-protecting, to guide without forcing, to help without domineering, and above all, to understand and respect the needs of this tiny precious person. We ask that Abe has all the benefits of a home in which two parents work together for the good of all concerned.

Grandmama's Blessing to Abe

May Divine bless you as you dedicate baby Abe.
So fresh from the Spirit plane.
He brings forth joy in our hearts.
So sweet, so innocent, so new.
Baby Abe is laughter and wonder, softness, and sweet lullabies.
But first and foremost, he is love.
As you guide him in the path of righteousness, remember the Divine is ever present.
Abe, may your parent's love be a force of blessings throughout all your days.

Aunt Lisa's Blessing to Abe

A baby keeps us in tune with the beauty in the world around us.
To wonder at birds and bright butterflies.

Delight at soft clouds that float through the skies.
Marvel at the water that splashes and flows.
Thrill at the feel of sand on bare toes.
The small things in life are discoveries of joy when seen through the eyes of a child.
Abe, may your life be blessed with discoveries and exciting adventures.

Uncle Patrick's Blessing

The greatest gift of all is the pleasure of a new baby with a smile as warm as sunshine's golden light.
With eyes, as bright as the twinkling Stars at night.
Abe, you are a miracle of creation of delight.
May your life be blessed with happiness and Divine manifestation.

Aunt Anne's Blessing

Baby Abe, somewhere at the time of your birth, a Star came down to Earth.
One new flower bloomed sweet and fair.
One new answer was given in prayer.
May this day of dedication be the beginning of a life filled with bountiful blessings.

Grandmama's Dedication

For as much as children are members of the collective consciousness of the highest aspect of each person, it is fitting that they receive blessings galore. We dedicate Abe to be raised in unity with vibrant health and abundant wealth in all forms for this is his birthright.

Kevin and Julie, you have taken upon yourselves an oath and a solemn responsibility to bring this child into the world. This responsibility involves a commitment from every member of the family to provide an atmosphere of love and respect.

Abe is blessed because he is in a home in which the principles of constructive thinking and love are being practiced. It is not enough to say you believe in the principles of love, for there must be a daily living of these in the home before the eyes of this child. Abe will grow to adopt this quality from what he sees put into practice. I will ask Abe's parents these questions for your consideration and response:

Julie and Kevin, do you pledge yourselves to surround this child with an atmosphere of Love?

Mama and Papa: We do.
Grandmama: Julie and Kevin, do you agree to keep yourselves and your conversation on the beautiful, happy, loving, and positive things of life to the best of your ability?
Mama and Papa: We do.
Grandmama: Julie and Kevin, do you agree to teach this child that he is the expression of the Supreme Source and has the right to expect in his body, his relationships, and his affairs all the blessings of the Divine?
Mama and Papa: We do.
Grandmama: Abe's parents will now offer advice to their infant son. Each parent will read one instruction in rotation.

Grandmama's Advice

Always remember to make life magical and relish the adventures and blessings of each day. Show your love in small thoughtful ways while you have the opportunity.
Let your loved ones know how important they are to you every day.
Treat yourself and all others with respect and gentle kindness.
Live the 'golden rule.' Do unto others as you would have them do unto you.
Be true to yourself, even if it means living outside the box.
Set your own standard regarding what defines your success and happiness.
Never let time go by without going within your heart center in quiet.
Never take life or love for granted.

Remember, when you are at the close of life, the most important thing is the depth of love shared with yourself and others.

Grandmama: What name have you chosen for this child?
Mama and Papa: Abe Rocky Garfield
Grandmama: Kevin and Julie, please affirm your pledge to Abe.
Mama and Papa: We pledge to each do our part in maintaining the environment of harmony and unconditional love in our home.

Kevin held Abe up like the father in the movie Lion King to symbolize offering his son's life to his destiny. The Spirit of the Lion Animal Totem truly lives in Abe. He is his baby sister Jay's protector. He demonstrates strength and determination.

Grandmama's Closing Prayer Intention

We make the prayer intention that Abe will always have a conscious awareness of the Divine's presence within. This shall manifest in good health, prosperity, and happiness. We dedicate Abe Rocky Garfield to the bounty of his mission fulfilled.

Abe Rocky Garfield, as your Grandmama, Reverend Patrice Joy, I proclaim that you embrace the presence of Divine Spirit as your Spirit, of Divine mind as your mind, and the eternal substance of Divine as your presence within. May the forces of light and love guide your choices. May harmony and hope fill your life. May the Angels guide your path by day and watch over you by night.

There are two important things a parent should give your child; one is roots and the other is wings. I speak for the family when I say Kevin and Julie, are two people who certainly know how to do this. And it is so.

Abe shared his second birthday with us on October 17, 2019. He loved sitting on the tractor and riding in his grandpa's gator that my husband, Dan, filled with straw. We simulated a hayride in the pick-up truck and went down the hill to Abe's aunt Lisa's to jump in the leaves and carve pumpkins. It brought back memories of Halloween fun with the whole family, enjoying pumpkin bread and warm apple cider.

Like Father – Like Son

Today you ask if Abe looks like you and I said, "No, not really, but he is like you in so many ways. He is charming, kind-hearted, fun-filled, magical, meticulous, intense, infectious, brilliant, constantly busy, but most of all loving. His strikingly good looks and magnetic personality will draw others to him throughout his life, just as you always have. As Abe grows older, I feel he will follow in your footsteps to facilitate change.

Abe is a peace builder and a servant leader. I once read "To be a true leader, one must learn to follow. These unique individuals have true security within and don't need to elevate themselves to prove it. A peacebuilder incorporates the quality of compassion and demonstrates empathy. They have the humane ability to understand the suffering of others and want to do something about it." He has two amazing parents to model the behavior and character traits of leadership and exceptional accomplishments.

The best part is Abe will do this in his own way, just as you both always have. He will influence others to have a better quality of life as he enjoys his day-to-day activities with full fervor. What a blessing he is to the lives he touches now and to those he will influence in the future. So many of the pictures of Abe are with him holding his arm around his little sister protectively. His kindness to her is shown daily and he is her faithful advocate.

My Granddaughter Jay Rocca

July 2020 brought another blessing to our family. Abe's little sister Jay Rocca was born on her cousin Cory's birthday. We are very connected to her in spirit and feel she is a high source of energy from the Stars. She is a bright, alert go-getter just like her parents, Julie and Kevin. Julie finished a major project online for her company during labor at 11:30 A.M. and delivered Jay at 4:30 P.M. just 2 hours after checking in at the hospital. I feel Mother Mary is directly connected to Jay's life and will be a guiding force as her special gifts are revealed.

I received a message in my morning meditations for Jay soon after she was born: Mother Mary told me Jay has special gifts and our family will guide her to develop leadership traits. She also related to me that Jay has chosen a unique calling to help women face their fears and find their special talents. Jay will receive messages from Mother Mary as her life unfolds to help her make decisions.

Jay is especially fond of turtles. Many times being drawn to a certain animal is an indication of the link with a person's Animal Totem. They may hold our life lessons. Turtles are associated with emotional depth and the Divine connection with our intuition. The Turtle represents the pacing of actions. Jay is a busy little girl., running here and running there. She may be like me and schedule too much activity in each day. Perhaps the Turtle will help her pace her undertakings as she gets older.

This is a letter I wrote to little Jay Rocca

Dear Baby Jay,

It won't be too long until I can hold you. In the meantime, I am cradling you in the arms of love and wrapping you in prayers for untold blessings. I saw light emitting from your Aura in the cute picture with your lovely Mommy. You have such a winsome charm to enchant others with your adorable cooing sounds and smile. I can't wait to see you and your big brother Abe in your joy-filled antics as you grow older. Incredible adventures await you both.

You have an amazing mother to show you how to be a liberated woman. She will demonstrate the qualities you will need to maintain your tender femininity and unique inner beauty. By demonstrating her strength, your mother, Julie, will inspire you to accomplish your dreams and uphold your calling. I saw a picture of you recently in which you have the same determined look on your face that your papa had as a baby. I am certain you will get what you go after.

Our family is so blessed to have such precious little ones. Your generation will lead us into changes that are meant to take place in our leadership roles to find World peace.

Until we are together, my love is all around you,
Grandmama

Jay Rocca – Our Cuddly Power-House

So adored are you *Baby Jay Bird*
Making the cutest sounds we've ever heard
We just want to hold you in our arms
And be delighted by your charms
You come to us from afar
Bringing the Light of a Star

You seem to be one who will watch and withhold
But when you get involved, you're a force to behold
Filled with the power from whence you came
Your special voice will be heard by those of fame
For you already know how to vocalize your unique sound
We look forward to learning the wisdom you've found

The light around your head depicts the light that you carry
Many will be blessed by the unique gifts you will be sharing
Teach us how to be fragile, but not frail
Gentle, but strong enough to prevail
I strive to be the kind of person who can help you grow
So that truth guides your path to help us honor the flow

My daughter Lisa is so talented with her writing and artistic abilities. She has such a talent for magically capturing the essence of a person in a creative art form. She has written several poems and stories honoring her nieces and nephews, but this one is my favorite.

Jay Bird, Written by Auntie Lisa

Pretty, pretty little Jay Bird
Tell me, tell me, what you heard
The wisdom in your eyes so bright
Like the keen observation of an owl at night
The loving inner strength of Mamma

The captivating fun and heart of Papa
You use your voice when it's needed
And again, if it needs to be repeated
You're Abe Rocky's baby sis
And Mamma and Papa's little miss
Your joy inside abounds
As you watch and look around
Pretty, pretty little Jay Bird
Tell me, tell me, what's the word?

We did Jay's Dedication Ceremony last Thanksgiving 2022. It was conducted in the same format as Abe's dedication service. Jay follows Abe's lead and he is such a good role model. Yet, she is such a little pacesetter herself. I feel Jay has two Animal Totems, the Turtle and the Blue Jay which is her nickname. She certainly has bold expression and communication is one of her strong points.

Patrick and Annie's new baby girl also had a dedication ceremony of love recently. Olive Elizabeth was born last September on Kevin's birthday after years of planning and preparation. She is truly our gift from the Divine and is a joyous bundle of personality galore. I felt during Annie's pregnancy that she was carrying a special child from the Angelic Realms. Olive is being raised he has much to teach us just as all the children do.

Our Angel Olive
Written by Grandmama 12-26-22

Your whimsical smile warms our heart
And has touched our souls right from the start
The Angels sent one of their own
To teach us about our true home
As you grow up cradled in your family's arms
We will continue to be endeared by your adoring charms
The Dove is your ally and Animal Totem leader
Bringing hope for each peace seeker

We cherish your genuine expression
For honesty is one of your lessons
Pure love is your gift to teach introspection
Bringing out our best heals all the rest

You're here to help all races become free
Kind acceptance is the key
You'll be an example of honoring our diversity
And a return to the world's sanity

Olive may demonstrate a connection to other Animal Totems as she gets older, but she does bring hope and joy to all those she meets. The Blue Bird of Happiness reminds us to fill the day with simple pleasures and brings assurance that even in hard times, things will be brighter. They are symbols of the Heavenly realm and bring messages of pure love. Olive is our family's Angel baby.

CHAPTER FOURTEEN
MEET MY THIRD GENERATION

Even though you love someone, it doesn't mean you are going to be able to spend your life near them. My granddaughter, Heather moved to Southern Mississippi and went to college in another part of the United States. She moved back with her dad and took her two older daughters Ava and Leah to California, and eventually back to the South again. She had a third daughter, little Natalie, and then a fourth daughter, Brently.

My life was vested in Ohio and Kentucky, getting a college degree and starting a Health Retreat. Then, life events took me to live in Georgia. Distance kept me from experiencing extended time with my great-granddaughters. Yet there are dreams I hold of my arms filled with wiggling little girls in the recollections of our visits together. I remember helping them set up a tea party when they visited me in Kentucky. It reminded me of tea parties I had with their uncles, Patrick and Kevin, Aunt Lisa, and cousin Cory in Ohio many years earlier. Here are poems I wrote for my previous great-granddaughters:

Cherished Memories of Times with My Granddaughters

Sit upon my knee. Ride the horsey and let me sing to you. You'll soon sleep to the lullaby that I sang to your mother Heather.

Beautiful Ava

Wow! What a doll!
No, I won't let you fall
The eyes of an angel you see
What a beauty you'll always be

Leah – My Little Bumble Bee

I'll bounce you 'trot a horse'
And leave with great remorse
You'll laugh with glee
Yes, upon my knee
What a little doll
So darling – so small
The fairies are your friends
The angels protect wherever your life leads

Ava demonstrates courage to explore the unknown like the Cat Animal Totem. She demonstrates its characteristics of intelligence, curiosity and a need for independence. Leah is our Bumble Bee. The Bumble Bee Animal Totem symbolizes hard work, diligence, and productivity. Leah holds all of these qualities.

Heather had two more incredible little girls Natalie and Brently. A baby Deer has been appearing around four-year-old Natalie's play area. The Deer Animal Totem teaches us to be kind, have gentle strength, and maintain a childlike innocence. These can be valuable lessons for Natalie to regulate her high levels of energy. I have had these same lessons.

Natalie said she felt Brently's Animal Totem is a Puppy. The Dog Spirit Animal teaches us to be loyal and love with all our hearts. Brently is almost two and time will tell if she will be like her cousins Dylan and Elliott and hold these qualities also.

When I went to Mississippi to conduct Tara's and Gary's wedding, I conducted a dedication ceremony for Leah and Natalie. I feel that Heather's four daughters are from the Fairy Realms and share good luck and blessings galore. The whole family is blessed with their mystical gifts. The following are poems that Lisa and I wrote for them:

Natalie – Child of Grace

Scamper, scamper, run, run
Oh, Natalie, you have such fun
Brought into this world to shine so bright

I see your incredible light
As you run, run little one
You'll do what needs to be done
Going from here to there
Touching others with your beauty so fair
Love is your gift to us
Even when you cause a fuss
Leaving others to clear the space
You'll continue to win every race
We love you dearly – our delightful little girl
Someday you'll be a woman of the world.
Run, run without a care
There is nothing you won't dare
When you are older, your wisdom begins to show
You'll take others into Divine's flow
The past and all its struggles will be gone
As you sing your lilting victory song

Brentley, Our Little Pixie Elf

Looking so somber and deeply intent
As if you have something to say
I wonder what your furrowed eyebrows meant
Until you laughed and giggled in carefree play
The elves claim you as their own
You like company
Content to be alone
Charming and cute as can be
Your pixie magic will bring many a friend
By your side, tried and true
Life will be fun-filled with the joy you send
Charmed with the fairy's morning dew
Yes, you are destined to be blessed
A survivor you'll always stay
Your future is filled with success
No matter what comes your way

In closing this chapter, I have more words of wisdom I'd like to share:
Always remember to make life magical and relish the blessings of each day.

If you don't take care of your needs, you won't have anything to give others.

Live the 'golden rule!' Do unto others as you would have them do unto you.

Be true to yourself, even if it means living outside the box.

Don't let anyone tell you what makes you successful and happy.

When you are at the close of life, all that is important is the love that you share.

CHAPTER FIFTEEN
TEACHING WHAT I LEARNED

Teaching Becomes My Learning Experience

They say we teach what we need to learn. I had programming and prejudice about my sexuality from the culture I grew up in. I have learned to respect the left and right brain qualities of both genders.

Introspect Your Parenting Patterns
Related to the Need to Develop Balanced
Male/Female Qualities

Inappropriate parenting can come from our parents, from society, or from one's attitude within. The absence of constructive role models sets up dysfunction. Being a kind, gentle, yet firm parent to oneself allows an individual to mature. They can function without guilt, blame, or defiance. Being the parent to oneself is the core concept in the psychological theory of Transactional Analysis (1964). Another primer for building self-esteem is Erick Berne's book entitled *Games People Play* (1961). He describes the ways we can live in denial and build distrust of ourselves and others.

Lack of training for one's personal responsibility cripples a child. When a child is sheltered from the consequences of their action, it fosters weakness and immaturity. If a person is sheltered from learning independence, growing up is difficult. Harsh treatment and punitive reprimands are equally destructive. Shame causes individuals to be shy and insecure, never trusting themselves or others to be strong and dependable.

Maturity requires a balance of self-love with the nurturing and guidance of a parent. A person cannot fully give to any relationship until they have learned to love and control themselves. They will be lost in playing denial games that negate another person's needs. Empathy is the capacity to see the other person's position and understand how your actions will affect them.

The immature person is incapable of this. A young child cannot see beyond his own immediate needs and desires. Prolonged immaturity in an adult becomes self-centered and can develop into narcissistic traits and a lack of regard for the needs of others. This is not to be mistaken for self-love.

Love for the inner child can thrive in people of all ages. An individual reaches his or her maturity by taking responsibility for their actions. Then the anger that accompanies past offenses can be cleared. Words spoken from repressed inner wounds and insecurity build walls, rather than bridges. The liberated whole is reconnected as the loving adult integrates kindness within.

The Role of Communication

Clear communication is vitally important in every form of relations. Romantic relationships are governed by these same principles. Two individuals who are withdrawn behind walls of fear will never totally experience one another. True commitment in a relationship is not about being there totally, or not at all. Power games of playing 'hard to get,' or being aloof or coy create insecurity. Mistrust results and can cause the other person to leave or hold on too tight. Power is given away when mates compare or compete with one another.

Balance is the foundation of an equalized relationship for good communication. This is characterized by connection and expression. There must be a willingness to be open so that communication comes from deep within the heart. This doesn't involve barriers, judgment, smothering, guilt projections, or expectations.

True communication between two people is based on spiritual communication. Loving-kindness comes from those who are pure of heart. Those who are attuned to the sacredness of all life listen to the voice in the Wind and the Water. They can hear the call to adventure and feel the mysteries of life. When this is shared with another person, depth of communication is attained. Creating a safe space for communication is the basis of success in any relationship. This completes the circle. No longer will two people make different worlds out of what is only one world.

I taught my family and clients that nonjudgmental communication can prevent rifts and buried emotions which end in passive-aggressive behaviors. Each person needs to tell the other what is in your heart. The people involved in buried interactions begin to resent each other and find faults. Picking at each other and criticism begins to undermine the trust at the core of the friendship. Then each person pulls away and spends less time with one another.

They are unaware of their motives and actions. Many people are unaware of their unconscious thoughts and motives. It is important to address unconscious subliminal communication in relationships. Many things are not put into words that are demonstrated in body language, voice tone, and attitude inference. Most people don't hear how they sound, but only how they intend to sound. We can live in the illusion of our version of true interactions. Listening well is the key to what you hear.

We are each individually in control of our destiny. What we put out acts like a boomerang and comes back into our lives as a blessing or a curse. We are a magnet drawing to us what we concentrate on. I have given a lot of thought and prayer to manifesting a happy merger with a mate based on loyalty and trust. Respect for one another's integrity is essential. Simplicity is a priority.

Love is In the Air

As you survey your life, tune back into the healing qualities of peace, love, joy, and harmony. Focus on the fulfillment they bring. Your body lets you know through your physical symptoms when and where there is trouble. Listen to your body's signals of trauma and emotional duress, and be more aware of your inner knowing.

You need this same awareness to deal with your relationships with others accurately. When you have lost the foundation of pure spiritual love in your relationships, you begin to have ways to compensate. Some people gamble compulsively; others drink excessively. Some overdo for others, and some run in all directions like I did.

Here is a helpful breathing technique for releasing inner turmoil: Inhale the quality of unconditional love to the count of five. Let go of anything that is troubling you on the exhale to the count of five. Find a place of silence inside yourself and retreat there peacefully. Dwell on unconditional love quietly for a few minutes. Then it will be easier to find peace with another person.

A physical place alone can trigger an energy that draws a person into past occurrences and events that happened there. A new job, new city, or a new attitude in your relationship can bring forth a 'New You'. When the heaviness of the past is released, the individual can become a liberated person. This state of liberation takes one to the wild nature that goes back to actual primal needs to find challenges and adventures. A wild thing can never be caged. The freedom lover searches for its kind.

Many times, I ended up alone with an immense untapped resource to offer a relationship. Eventually, I became this self-sustained person who could live happily in a single role since I found wholeness within.

Stay in Touch with Your Better Self

Your level of contentment and fulfillment depends on the way you choose to invest your time. As the day closes, do you feel the time has been well spent to take care of yourself and bring happiness into your world? Are you focusing on actions, attitudes, and thoughts that make life a joyful experience? Are there things you need to let go to have a restful night of restoring sleep? Let Divine love fill your heart and you can begin to drift off into a restful sleep.

The world holds many miracles awaiting us if we are open-minded enough to consider new possibilities of the healing power of love. The feelings of being loved and appreciated are a basic part of healing. Self-love is the foundation for recovery from all kinds of pain, whether emotional, mental, or physical. Getting to know yourself and respecting who you are no matter what others in your environment are telling you are the keys. Here are a few of the things I do to continue to love myself and to be authentic:

Be inner-directed with self-love. Embrace the spiritual awareness of being the quality of unconditional love with yourself and with others. Forgiveness is the path to finding this healing quality within. Here is my self-care plan:

Concentrate on what is right with you instead of what is wrong.

Imagine yourself in a blessing bubble.

List three things you are grateful to have in your life.

Give five compliments to yourself every day.

Give five compliments to others every day.

Say I love you while looking in the mirror every day.

List things you like to do and do them.

Defined what is important in a relationship.

How would you define yourself as you review the seasons of your life?

An emancipated, free-spirited individual will never be content with archaic male/female roles. Both men and women of this nature are free, fun-loving, sensual, and romantic. In a relationship between two liberated people, a life is sought in which time is spent in fulfilling activities. The multi-variated interests of each are pursued. A balance of closeness and space for each individual is a requirement. Compromise is the priority. These are the qualities I found in myself and the values I want to model. This is what I have chosen to draw into my life in a relationship. But first, I had to find peace in myself.

CHAPTER SIXTEEN
BRINGING IT ALL TOGETHER

Being True to Myself

My spiritual experiences and meditations were just as important in my recovery as my medical findings and psychological awareness. So, where does all this take us? How did we get from there to here? It feels like I have lived my life on the edge many times getting by on a wing and a prayer. I began to realize that although I could live alone and be happy, I prefer to enjoy life with my ultimate mate. I didn't want to label all men based on my past experiences. I got some advice in meditation regarding this process of finding a spiritual union.

Advice from my Guardian Angel

Don't let the fear of what might be, destroy what could be.
Don't let what you think you know get in the way of what you can learn

The Qualities of the Mate I Choose to Share My Life Experiences

I had to leave behind the dysfunctional patterns of my past so that I could reach the joy in my soul. I chose to go to the laughter within to find peace and resolution. With persistence and resilience, soul wounds can become soul songs. My family has been my inspiration. I was able to find within myself what I had been seeking in others. Almost eight years ago, I finally felt ready to have a man in my life and still maintain balance within.

I pondered my description of the ideal mate. This combines the male/female adult and the child aspect of a person. It incorporates all ages. It unites the curiosity and spontaneity of youth and the wisdom of age. This enables me to go through life's hardships without becoming embittered by it all. My ideal mate's life is spent loving the magic of the moment with an attitude that each day holds a wonderful secret to be found and shared. He works on his personal growth and evolution. He honors all living beings and lives humbly in Oneness. He loves himself, his parents, and the Divine within. He knows what is most important. We are to each work on ourselves. It is not about us fixing one another. You can't fix anyone else and shouldn't even try. I want my mate to be happy, but I can't give this gift to him, and he can't give it to me.

My ideal mate respects his sacred self and is inner-directed.

My ideal mate is kind-hearted, mystical, sexy, and full of fun.

My ideal mate shares compatible priorities, interests, and beliefs.

My ideal mate is health-conscious and respects his body's needs.

My mate loves himself and me enough to live in the flow of the Divine's highest plan for our life together. My mate and I will have wonderful times and other times that may not be up to our expectations. Some things may be inconvenient. Some days may be rough, but we can ride them out with teamwork. We both need to heal all fear-based patterns and motivation to establish truth and clarity. At times, life may present hurdles. It is about getting over them together that counts. It isn't the big thing that kills a relationship. It is the small things that are left unresolved. We'll stick it out and work on any kinks together. We'll build bridges, not walls.

Affirmations and Goals for My Optimal Relationship

I have a mate in my life who is willing to work together to build stepping stones to healthy communication and mutual understanding.

I have an intimate relationship built on honesty and transparent communication.

My mate and I have joyful and quiet times lingering under the blue sky as we enjoy nature living in our dream home in the woods.

My mate and I listen to what is important to one another.

My mate and I focus on what is good about one another and remember the mutual attraction that drew us together initially and sustained our continual bliss.

My mate and I spend time loving and laughing and supporting one another emotionally with compassion.

My mate and I have the safety of an open-hearted relationship based on Divine unconditional love, peace, and honesty.

My mate and I handle difficulties together as equal partners.

My mate and I enjoy sunsets and the Stars at night together.

The Ultimate Relationship

I have come to an awareness that love is not earned by perfect behavior. The individuals must wipe the slate of past grievances. Then, failures of past relationships are not projected on this new union. Each partner has a special role in your growth. You need to remain centered in peace rather than fluctuate in mercuric highs and lows.

Life can be enhanced by sharing joys and tough times. Keeping the happy inner child alive is critical to a union filled with light-hearted fun. A man-child treasures the jewel of a woman who has also kept the spirit of her youth. This woman-child flourishes with a strong playmate who enjoys the adventure of the dance of life. Cherishing one another as much as the breath that sustains life is the key to this union.

Trusting without naivety is the quality that enables discernment of the selection of a compatible partner. The longevity of this union comes with honesty and faith. Support of each other dreams and continual comfort builds a world of laughter and joy to share. A sacred place is created between the individuals. Both honor this as hallowed ground, not to be intruded upon by anything hurtful.

Both maintain a sanctuary, a safe harbor to retreat from the pressure of the outside world. A place where the self is uplifted, justified, and acknowledged. Each partner will find one other person who continually believes in him or her, no matter what. A haven is formed to rest and restore before going back into the daily grind of the outside world, a place where acceptance and understanding reign.

I found this relationship in my mid-70s. It is never too late. The following poems describe the mature love and bliss that is based on friendship. I wrote these poems to express my feelings when I met Dan – My Bear Man.

Against All Odds

We met against all odds.
Who could have planned it?
We met as our eyes talked.
Perhaps dreams do become reality.

Hello Again

It seems I know you
I feel one heart between the two
Our eyes connect- spirits soar
But we haven't met before
This time and another
No longer to look further
I wonder if he thinks of me
No division, walls, or chains I see
For ours is magic of words spoken
Now as before, the chain is unbroken
You touched me and sparks fly
My hope soars to the sky
You are at the core of all I hold dear in my heart.
Spirit answers "You're been together since the start."

I'll Meet You There

In my dreams, there is a place I see you
Let's get together
I'll meet you there
Where I am held in your arms
Feelings of love encircle me
Our love is pure and true
Ecstasy – soaring free
Complete understanding without words
Together in heaven with you at my side
Our bodies and spirits merge
As though no others exist
Let's get together. I'll meet you there

True Love Abides

Our magical union is nothing like what I have experienced before on this earth. I feel we came from the Stars and finally reached the point in our soul growth to spend the rest of eternity together. Destiny has a way of unfolding, and the fairy tale came true. Dan and I both have memories of a life together as American Indians and a lifetime in Ireland and England. I feel we were Druids together.

In our current life, we married the weekend of Thanksgiving 2018 to symbolize the gratitude we feel for one another. In a sacred American Indian ceremony, we joined our lives as husband and wife in a retreat center in the Kentucky woods. Our log home in the forest provided a sanctuary to expand our love and spiritual enlightenment as we started the journey to share eternity through the realms.

I've found a man who measures up to my dad. Dan has a special connection to the trees and animals. He has such a gentle spirit and has been embraced by my family. My daughter spiritually adopted Dan as her father and calls him Dad. My sons have all expressed their love for him as well and have introduced him as their dad.

My wonderful husband Dan and I retired and moved South in May 2021. We begin our day with coffee by the lake and close the day enjoying the Star-filled sky. Dan built a dock and goes fishing in his john boat. He set up a tool center in the garage and loves working with wood. As a Nature lover, he enjoys making improvements on our land.

We established several healing centers throughout our incredible property to pray for personal, family, and world healing. I am dedicated to my studies of Inner-Realm Travel. We cherish time with one another and express gratitude often. The vibrant colored Flowers in our Hope Garden bring healing to my soul. We have two statues in this area: a little boy and a girl who remind us to maintain our playful nature and to take care of our little inner child. The boy is fishing, and the girl holds a crystal in her upturned palms.

Our mystical Forest calls us to the Woods daily. On one of our walks in the Forest, we found two giant Trees that were connected at the base. One of them is a Pine Tree, and the other is a huge Oak Tree. We cleared the area around them and set up a Sanctuary to honor our Twin Spirits. We also did ceremonies to dedicated centers for gratitude, grieving, self-care, and the Center for Universal Truth. We both pledged to continue to pray for peace Worldwide in our World Peace Center. The Grandmother Tree and Grandfather Tree connect us to the wisdom of our lineage through time.

Sharing my love of Nature with Dan brings joy to my heart. We sit in the Woods filled with Pine Trees and Ferns in our Tree Cove Prayer Center. A small statue of Mother Mary, Joseph, and Jesus in the nativity scene gives solace. It symbolizes the balance of the highest masculine and feminine qualities, which are compassion, mercy, nurturing, creativity, mental clarity, wisdom, and gentle strength. Baby Jesus symbolizes the miracles of unconditional love.

Dan and I have a Feather in our Communication Center. My American Indian friends taught us to pass this back and forth if we disagree. The one holding the feather is the only one who is to speak. This allows all parties to completely speak their mind in the verbal conflict. The focus is on using respectful words and listening to one another. Reiki, Sound, Breath, and Color Healing Sessions, Spirit Journeys, and Tuning Fork Ceremonies are becoming regular activities in our Meditation Sanctuary filled with Gemstones and family pictures. We have trips planned to the East and West Coast to enjoy time with our families.

I visualize us all enjoying excellent health each day. I wrote this poem to express what my path has shown me about love.

The Meaning of Love

What is love?
Love is living
The joy of giving
Honesty you see
Freedom to just be
Gladness in sharing
Kindness and caring

The Seasons of Life

The seasons of a person's life correlate to the calendar's seasons which bring change. Spring offers the time for the budding of new possibilities (youth and puberty); summer brings warm lazy days to relax after the planting process (mid-life age 40-50); fall is the harvest of one's investment of efforts (in your sixties); winter is the slowing down of old age (seventy and on). Each season of life has its pleasures and pain. It is up to the individual to accomplish what is truly important. Find the priorities before the clock gives us its warning toll that time is running out.

Life unfolds in circles of reconnection. We start childhood in a co-dependent bonding process with our immediate family unit and community. This may be a positive experience or one that creates a void. Nevertheless, as an individual gets older, there comes a time of nostalgia and a desire to return to one's roots. The seasons of growth are the story one creates to reveal the drama or peace that has unfolded within.

There are cycles of activity in which the individual seeks fulfillment in a variety of ways. This is expressed in relationships, career accomplishments, and the accumulation of things. When the things that surround the person become boring or cluttered, a sense of detachment and loneliness sets in. This leads to a point of searching for a deeper meaning in life.

If a person doesn't look beyond the mental fixation of circular thoughts, the pattern of hiding from oneself leads to stress, illness, and disappointment. Superficial relations and an overload of activities are ways to develop the story, but these are never the answer to true self-fulfillment.

The circles and cycles continue to lead in a downward spiral as the opportunity to learn keeps presenting itself, in the same recurring type of self-victimization and abusive relationships. The person gets lost in the accumulation of things or finds the next dilemma and responds repeatedly in the same cycle of self-destruction. The seasons of growth involve lessons learned from all these efforts.

Hopefully, you have considered what your time has been devoted to as the seasons of your life change. What has been brought into being by the seasons of life that you chose? I have worked with individuals who are losing their quality of life. It is so tragic when a person outlives the ability to enjoy the minutes of the life they have remaining. Choose to rise above the circumstances and find the joy that each day offers.

My Soul Contract

I agreed to be present in the here and now. I agreed to abide in the place of trust and forgiveness. I agree to believe in my worth and honor the Divinity in myself as in all forms of life. I agree to bring Light to Earth to establish true peace within humanity.

Stepping-Stones for Growth

I have moved beyond the stereotyping of the era I was raised in and the resulting beliefs about marriage and myself. My upbringing taught a woman's job is to raise the children and a man's job is to earn money. I've reached a time in my life when I stopped external control and co-dependency.

I spent my life going in circles to get the approval of others. I was brought up believing that other people's feelings and their happiness were my responsibility. I had to work at deep levels to stop co-dependency which was lodged in my subconscious.

My self-value was so low, others could control me. Threats of loss have been empty words used to control my actions and to persuade me to do what others wanted. I have also learned that some people will say what you want to hear with no intention of doing as promised. I have accepted that my role in these past interactions was to be a victim to get attention. I was messing up my own life to get the pity my mother had confused with love. This is one of the patterns I have left behind.

My goal is to continue to improve my health as I get older. I have established the intent to feel peaceful and calm throughout my daily activities. I am committed to doing the things I enjoy. I love reading, listening to music, meditating, and walking in nature with Dan. Visiting with family whenever possible is one of my primary pleasures. I accept that I am an individual who demonstrates real strength of spirit. I experience the joy of fulfillment in my life. This can act as a mirror and offer the opportunity for others to find the tools to establish their own joy, peace, and good health.

The Encounters of My Mind

The experience of childhood encounters challenged me to bring forth my strongest traits of survival to find personal empowerment. I feel it is my privilege to use the wisdom gained and hope to be a guide for others in similar situations. I had to leave self-condemnation, remorse, regret, and victim patterns in the past. These painful experiences are over, and I must avoid recreating them in my head and new relationships. I accept that I am not bound by the process of my growth.

I can turn these events into stepping stones for growth and new awareness. I am still faced each day with the option of moving in a positive direction of personal growth and healing. The choice of recovery remains mine. What direction will I choose? I have reminded my children and my students that progress requires practice. Through repetition, new habits are instilled and improved until they become natural unconscious reactions. It takes courage to dare to take risks. Sometimes one must try and try again to accomplish the chosen result.

Never again will there be closed chambers of regret which I hide. The light floods in the window of my soul warming my inner child with delight. Now I see with a higher perspective connected with pure intention. Unconditional love is the key that opened the doors to the inside of me. I can wander through unexplored places in my mind that I closed in my childhood. My inner guidance has opened uncharted realms that provide answers and treasures to behold.

Planetary Healing

Personal relationships are a model for planetary relations. We can come to this true union as a planet when all the individuals reconnect with this pure love. Then our hearts will beat with the Universal heartbeat and all will live in harmony. This union was disrespected when humanity cut themselves off from the blessings of the Divine. Many used their gift of free will to separate from the good that they could receive.

Unconditional love is God's constant presence. I have come to realize that no harsh judge and jury is punishing us for our sins. Each person creates a unique set of events, which separates or unites him or her with the awareness of Unconditional Love. We are each being taken through the clearing of past grievances so we can reconnect with our empowerment, and destined prosperity and purpose. Many had misused power to oppress others in past lives and other realms. Individuals deny themselves control and power in their current life situation as a function of self-condemnation and guilt for suffering caused previously.

The priority of self-acceptance and forgiveness changes the motivation from getting ahead in this world to getting in touch with the internal essence of One's self. Bringing this inner calm into all relationships and experiences is the healing of our planet. As the true presence of love emerges, it seems there is a return to the purity and innocence of the happy child deep within all of us. The spontaneity of this expression of our greatest hopes and dreams brings everything that makes life worth living. Two can share this when each respects the other's space. Each person operates out of the place of acceptance that spreads pure love.

When forgiveness takes over, we no longer need to punish ourselves and others. Forgiveness from others is directly related to the amount one gives. What is done to one is done to all. When judgment is replaced by acceptance, peace will reign on Earth.

I want to express that nothing in life needs to hold a person back. I always had encouragement and helping hands on my path from my spiritual guidance. I always made enough money to get by. The close members of my family have faced hardships including anorexia kidney failure, heart attacks, drugs, alcoholism, stroke, back surgery, hip replacement surgery, arthritis, autoimmune liver disease, life-threatening skin cancer, bi-polar disorders, autism, schizophrenia, multiple-personality disorder, severe PTSD, infertility, physical and emotional abuse, and even death. It's not like we didn't have challenges. Mother used to say, "When the going gets tough, the tough get going."

During my adventures, I got in touch with the adult I am, the Light Healer and the magical child within me. I have kept my inner child alive through the hurtful experiences life presented. I think the most important thing in my life quest is that I found my True Self, I can express my worth. I found I am my own best friend and found friends of a feather to share life and love with me.

The book *Braiding Sweetgrass* by Robin Wall Kimmerer touched my life immensely. She teaches Indigenous Wisdom and scientific knowledge in such delightful stories that relate her life lessons from the plants and world of nature. This parallels the impact nature has had in guiding my life lessons.

Ashley Judd said something that summarizes my life as well as hers. "I did my best and it was good enough." I would like to quote Robert Frost when he said, "In three words I can sum up everything I've learned about life; It goes on."

I recently read Patt Lind-Kyle's book entitled *Embracing the End of Life: A Journey into Dying and Awakening*. It has impacted me at a turning point. I have been in a life review since our move to Georgia. I am facing another phase of life. Perhaps my last. How long will this final chapter be? Who knows?

I want to completely awaken before I cross over in a smooth transition to the other side. I feel this book has given me the tools to experience my life and death more fully. I recommend it for those of all ages to live more abundantly in the precious present moment. I used the following plan that I had given my clients and combined it with Kyle's life review practices to clear any mental and emotional debris that I was still carrying from the past. If you keep reliving past traumas, they become present traumas.

I am 80 years old and facing another phase of life. I feel this will involve less 'doing' and more 'being'. Perhaps being in the flow is what this journey is all about anyway!

Stress does not exist in the present moment. Stress is the byproduct of worrying about what did happen or what could happen as a result of this. Make the intention to clear your mind and simplify your lifestyle. As you learn to put your attention on your breathing, you can have better mental focus and be more organized. You can have better sleep, improved health, and emotional benefits as well. Be aware of yourself and all your senses at the present time to have a better memory and ability to handle stress. In the following process, hold the intention to go within to find inner peace. Clear your mind of stagnant thoughts and your lungs of stagnant air with these breath routines:

1. Breathe rapidly through the nose inhaling and exhaling with a shallow breath to cleanse repetitive thoughts and behaviors. Imagine you are burning off these old problems and response patterns.

2. Close your eyes and inhale deeply to the count of four. Fill with the energy of unconditional love. Exhale to the count of seven and let go of everything else.

3. Open your eyes and stare at a spot directly in front of you. Let your eyes relax and close them again. Imagine a restful scene in nature. Experience all the colors, sounds, and fragrances. Fully enjoy the peace of this moment in time.

4. Begin to slowly count backward from ten to one. Breathe gently as you imagine you are sinking deeper and deeper into your heart center of unconditional love within. Rest in this peaceful state of being.

5. Count to five and gradually return in your awareness to your physical body. Move your fingers and toes as you return to the 'ever-present now'.

At the Close of My Life

When my time on Earth is in the final chapter, I want to be someone who brings a smile to others. I want them to feel better about themselves because I hope to have touched their lives. I want to be thought of as a good listener who truly hears the 'heart cry' of those with whom I come in contact. I chose to be an inspiration to encourage others to reach their life goals and dreams.

Regarding My Relationships

I allow myself to be open and vulnerable. I conduct my interactions with faith in Divine protection. I only form relationships with people who act with integrity and empathy. I encourage others to see the worth in themselves. As an authentic leader, I want to be an effective healthy living role model.

My Ultimate Life Goals

In my search, I want to have lived the essence of my true identity. I chose to let my heart lead me to the realm of Oneness. I am a part of the awakening of truth and peace on a personal and global level. I am a candle flame to shine forth light and joy in the world.

At the close of my life, I want to have lived, loved and laughed every day, and appreciated the precious moments given to each person. I want what I have invested my time in to be well worth the cost. I want to be able to say that I lived my life in service. I gave the best I had and saw the light of goodness in the hearts of others. I motivated others by my passion to act for the greater good of myself and others. I loved and lived to the fullest and served those I met along the way. And what did I learn through it all? As I once heard. "Everything matters and nothing matters!"

My Final Words of Advice

If I can leave you with any words of advice, it would be these: Always remember to make life magical and relish the adventures and blessings of each day. Show your love in small thoughtful ways while you have the opportunity. Every day let your loved ones know how important they are to you. Treat them with respect and gentle kindness. Open up and allow yourself to be vulnerable. Never let time go by without expressing how much you care. Be grateful for all the little and the big things you have accomplished. Especially, be grateful for those who love you. Never take love for granted.

I hope I have instilled the belief that a higher power is leading and protecting you as your life path unfolds. Go within your heart center in quiet time, if only a few minutes each day, so that the busy world will not cause you to forget the priority of unconditional love. May the forces of light and love guide your choices and may hope and harmony fill the precious moments of every day.

OTHER BOOKS AVAILABLE BY REV. PATRICE JOY, MA

The Healing Feeling Children Series:

Book One: Meet the Sprinklets and Pestlets

Book Two: The Sprinklets and Pestlets Take Over Earth

Book Three: Teddy the Turtle's Family and Friends

Book Four: Teddy, Bonnie, and the Bullies

Book Five: Play Potentials Booklet

Book Six: Practical Life Skills & Related Research

Sprinklet Self-awareness Cards

Friends Forever

Buffy Meets Lucky Learning How To Make Friends

Dolphins Dreaming Our Planetary Healing

BIBLIOGRAPHY

Amen D. (1998). *Change Your Brain Change Your Life*. New York, NY, Penguin Press.

Assouline S. & Lupkowski, A. (2003) – *Developing Mathematical Talent: A Guide for Challenging and Educating Gifted Students*. Austin, TX. Prufrock Press.

Benson, H. & M. Klipper (1975). *The Relaxation Response*. New York, NY, Avon Books.

Berne, E. (1964). *Games People Play.* New York, NY, Penguin Press.

Bruch, H. M.D. (1978). *The Golden Cage.* Cambridge, MA, University Press.

Childre, Doc, & Martin, H. & Beech, D. (1999). *The Heartmath Solution.* San Francisco, Ca, HarperCollins, Publishing.

DeBono, E. (1967). The *5-Day Course in Thinking.* New York, NY, Penguin Press.

Farmer, S. (20040 *Power Animals: How to Connect with Your Spirit Guides,* Carlsbad, CA, Hay House Inc.

Freed, A. (1974). *TA for Tots.* Englewood Cliffs, NJ, Jalmar Press.

Harris, T. (1969). *I'm OK, You're OK.* New York, NY, Harpers and Row Pub.

Kyle, Patt-Lind, MA. (2017*). Embracing the End of Life: A Journey into Dying and Awakening.* Woodbury, MN. Llwellyn Publications,

Kimmer, Robin Wall (2013) *Braiding Sweetgrass.* Minneapolis, Minn., Milkweed Editions Publishers

Kyle, Patt-Lind, MA. (2010). *Heal your Mind, Rewire Your Brain.* Santa Rosa, CA. Energy Psychology Press

Lawlis, F. M.D. (2006). *The IQ Answer.* New York, NY, Penguin Group Press.

Longstreth, E. (2011). *Joy in Wealth.* College Station, TX, Virtual bookworm Pub.

Maloney, M. M.D. & Kranz, R. (1991). *Straight Talk About Eating Disorders.* New York, NY, Bantam Double Day Publishing.

Maltz, M. (1960). *Psycho-cybernetics.* New York, NY, Prentice Hall Inc.

McCarthy, J. & Kartzinel, J. (2009). *Healing and Preventing Autism*: New York, NY: Penguin Press.

Pemberton, Lois (1948). *The Stork Didn't Bring You*: New York, Hermitage Press.

Sarno, J. (1991). *Healing Back Pain: The Mind-Body Connection*, New York, NY: Warner Books Inc.

Smith L. (1976). *Improving your Child's Behavioral Chemistry*, Hoboken, NJ: Prentice Hall.

Kimmel, H. (2001). *A Girl Named Zippy.* Portland Oregon, *Broadway Books.*

ABOUT THE AUTHOR

Rev. Patrice Joy, MA is a licensed minister and has over forty years of experience in the field of education, business, family dynamics and Integrative Health. Her educational degrees from Antioch McGregor University are a Bachelor of Arts with a double major in Health and Wellness and Human Development and a Master of Arts in Community Change and Civic Leadership. As a Reiki Master Instructor and Herbal Master, she utilizes several forms of vibrational medicine. Rev Patrice has taught at Webster University and Forest Park Community College. She was the first woman hired in territorial sales management for the Xerox Corporation and was the hostess of the TV Series entitled The Parent's Role. She conducted programs for several government agencies including CASA, Head Start, Salvation Army, Fresh Start, and One Stop. Rev. Joy's favorite workshops were presented for USAF Falcon Trail Youth Camp, USAFA Family Advocacy, Boy Scouts, and Older Moms Coalition. Rev. Patrice was voted Woman of the Year in the Women's Professional Organization in 2011/2012. Her leadership skills have led her to the founding of several companies including Creative Learning Programs, Western Celebrations, Sisters of Safety Non-profit,

Seekers of Serenity (SOS) Nonprofit, Harmonizing Health Retreat, and Harmonizing Health Wisdom. The content in her writing is based on the concept that a calm mind and relaxed body have more life energy. Techniques are presented to learn self-control and gain freedom from destructive emotions of guilt, anger, and depression. Improved health of mind, body, and spirit creates better relationships and productivity. The foundation of her work is peace, harmony, and joy within and in our world. More available books at www.harmonizinghealthwisdom.com

.

www.ingramcontent.com/pod-product-compliance
Lightning Source LLC
Chambersburg PA
CBHW031546040426
42452CB00006B/206